More Pit Ghosts,
Padfeet & Poltergeists

More Pit Ghosts, Padfeet & Poltergeists

by
Liz Linahan

𝕿𝖍𝖊 𝕶𝖎𝖓𝖌'𝖘 𝕰𝖓𝖌𝖑𝖆𝖓𝖉 𝕻𝖗𝖊𝖘𝖘

1996

More Pit Ghosts Padfeet & Poltergeists is published by
The King's England Press, 21, Commercial Road, Goldthorpe Indus-
trial Estate, Goldthorpe, Rotherham, South Yorkshire S63 9BL
Typeset in 11pt Palatino on 13 point by The Local History Press.

ISBN 1 872438 13 X

Contents

Foreword

It was more than twenty years ago when my interest in the paranormal was first triggered by stories I was told by my grandparents as a child. They were a solid down-to-earth working class couple born and brought up at the turn of the century in the heart of South Yorkshire's then bustling industrial heartland. But despite the harshness of life during two world wars and a depression, with poverty and unemployment on every street of terraced houses, there was always time for story telling - particularly about ghosts, goblins and things that went bump in the night. Haunted houses, spirit rapping, Spring Heeled Jack, the park ghost, and the Boggard of Bunting Nook - these were just some of the supernatural terrors my grandmother recalled from her childhood in Sheffield.

I remembered listening at her knee as she described how, in her mother's day, that is, the late 19th century, parts of the city had been terrorised by this ghost who was able to make huge leaps over walls and fences.

"It was said he had springs on his boots and he just appeared in front of people - mostly women on errands - scaring them out of their wits", she told me.

On one occasion, gangs of men and police officers chased the strange visitor through the streets of Pittsmoor but he managed to escape by performing a breath-taking leap over the gates of Burngreave Cemetery.

"They never caught him and it never came out who it was, so people came to believe he was not of this world", said my grandmother.

Then she would go on to tell stories about Long Sammy, the Duke of Darnall and other long lost characters from Sheffield's past.

Years later, when I tried to believe six impossible things before breakfast I was inspired to check out the wonderful story I had heard as a child. But I drew a blank. There appeared to be few written records about Spring Heeled Jack and his reign of terror in Victorian Sheffield. Although it was clear stories like this were the very stuff of popular tradition and entertainment, those who wrote the newspapers of the day found rustic tales unworthy of record as real "history."

Ghost stories to them were just frivolous distractions from the working day and the things ordinary decent Christian folk were supposed to spend time thinking about. Today in these more enlightened times, some of us have come to realise that oral tradition is just as

7

important as the official history - if not more so because it records what ordinary people felt and believed not just about this world but the otherworld, the world of the spirit. Unfortunately, this realisation has come at a time when the tight knit communities which generated this great body of folklore, belief and superstition, are disappearing.

Nowadays, kids don't tend to sit round the hearth listening to grandparents and other tribal elders telling them tales about their ancestors and land. The tales which gave their village or town an identity are not being passed on to future generations because youngsters are more interested in computer games, videos and other high tech distractions. This is why collections of stories like those contained in this book are so important if we are not to lose contact with the tales, beliefs and superstitions which made us what we are. Liz Linahan has performed what many other authors in this field have failed to do - that is, gone out in the field and recorded stories which are still told in villages and hamlets of Northern England. Together with her previous work, *Pit Ghosts, Padfeet and Poltergeists*, this volume is a welcome addition to the small but growing list of alternative history books which this region needs so much.

David Clarke
Sheffield, February 1996.

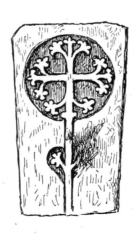

Introduction

In 1994, I travelled around South Yorkshire collecting first-hand accounts of the supernatural from ordinary people, which formed the basis for *Pit Ghosts, Padfeet and Poltergeists*. The stories I used were told to me by people who had perhaps only ever had one unexplained experience in their lives. Some remained sceptical of the supernatural, while others were convinced that, alongside everyday existence, a darker, inexplicable side to life often reveals itself. Rather than ending with the publication of *Pit Ghosts*, so many tales were forthcoming that there were soon enough for a second book.

More Pit Ghosts Padfeet and Poltergeists is the result of an ongoing collection of local stories from South Yorkshire, and its bordering counties of north Nottinghamshire and Derbyshire. Haunted pubs and churches, phantom coaches and inexplicable 'fairy lights' feature along with tales of witchcraft, UFO's and, of course, pit ghosts and poltergeists. Historic buildings and ancient sites are included alongside first-hand accounts of hauntings in ordinary council houses, combined with local legends and beliefs which paint an altogether different picture of this haunted county.

Once again I am indebted to the residents of South Yorkshire who shared their experiences with me, for without their co-operation, this second book could never have been completed.

Publisher's note: The "occult" is a strange and difficult concept for some people. We *strongly* urge anyone who may be tempted to dabble in such matters to desist immediately. If you feel troubled in any way by subjects covered in this book, we strongly recommend you consult a clergyman or some other qualified spiritual advisor. We cannot accept any responsibility.

The Oaks Colliery Disaster, Barnsley, as seen by a contemporary artist. The frequency of terrible accidents contributed both to the miners' sense of community and to the dark folklore of terrible things happening underground.

10

More Pit Ghosts,
Padfeet And Poltergeists

Following Pit Ghosts, Padfeet and Poltergeists, this chapter serves to update the growing collection of stories concerning some of Yorkshire's most unwelcome inhabitants: colliery ghosts, encountered by men at work underground since well before this century; the mythical black Padfoot hound, feared as a harbinger of doom and yet revered as a protector of the lonely traveller; and finally, the noisy and disruptive poltergeist, which can make its presence felt in the most unexpected places...

Pit Ghosts

'A mile from Rotherham be veri goode pittes for cole,' wrote the traveller Leland, crossing through South Yorkshire in the reign of Henry VIII. Much later in history, when coal mining had grown into one of the principal industries in South Yorkshire, new recruits were terrified by older miners' tales of what they may encounter when alone underground. Many of the collieries which were productive until quite recently featured shafts of a great age, such as Caphouse in Barnsley, and poor safety precautions in mines of old meant that pits were sites of frequent disaster. Some of the oldest collieries were worked for several generations, continually being expanded and updated. Many pits consequently featured horror stories of pre-1900's spectres alongside sightings of a more modern nature.

Searching for new stories of haunted pits was not an easy task, especially since widespread pit closure throughout the county has rendered tales of pit ghosts no more than fireside anecdotes, which will fade and die with the passage of time. However, there are many excolliers who still remember their own experiences vividly, and several new stories are included below to augment the wider selection in *Pit Ghosts, Padfeet and Poltergeists.*

Markham Colliery

Ron Webster was a Chesterfield-based miner for many years, and had an experience while underground at Chesterfield's Markham Colliery which remains clear in his memory to this day.

Many years ago when pit ponies were still in use for coal transportation, they were stabled in underground stalls and tended to by a 'hosler' or 'osler', who fed and watered them, and generally took responsibility for them when the shifts were over. Markham's osler was a man named Archie, who, after many years' service, died suddenly in the stables. Ron Webster was underground in an area close to the stables shortly after Archie's death, when he looked towards the ponies and noticed a figure feeding them... and a closer look revealed that it was Archie!

Markham Colliery was also reputedly haunted by the ghost of a deputy who always appeared in a flooded area of the mine where drainage pumps were installed. Many of the miners refused to venture into this area alone; the pumps needed to be activated at regular intervals, and sightings of the phantom deputy standing in a corner and watching them at work were common.

Cortonwood Colliery

In the mid-1970's a teenage apprentice at Cortonwood, Barnsley, was working underground in a secluded area when he noticed somebody he at first thought to be one of his colleagues, emerging from a coal face. The lad was puzzled as he believed that nobody should have been present in this area of the pit. Curiously he watched the figure emerge, until it became clear that it was clothed in outdated uniform, with an old-fashioned square helmet and gaiters and knee-pads. Suddenly afraid, he ran quickly to his colleagues who checked the area on his insistence but found nothing. The young man was made the butt of several jokes as his fellow miners refused to take his sighting seriously... until a short while later, when it was revealed that this very coal face was adjacent to an underground working of the nearby Lundhill Colliery, in which a tragic accident had killed several miners in the 1850's.

The Prince Of Wales, Pontefract

This public house, close to the race course at Castleford, would seem an unlikely place for the appearance of a colliery ghost, and indeed, many people who have walked past a certain photograph which hung on one of the walls until quite recently, had no idea of the origin of the mysterious face which was visible between two hydraulic chocks. Taken many years ago at a West Yorkshire colliery, the photographer believed that he had taken an underground view of some of the older workings of the pit... until the photograph was developed, and a ghostly face, resplendent in an old-fashioned helmet and headlamp, became visible in one corner of the photograph. Sadly, the photograph was removed when previous tenants left the premises, and the identity of the ghostly miner will always remain a mystery.

Glasshoughton Colliery

Mr Matt Kitchen, a former West Yorkshire collier, recalls being told the following tale by a friend who had worked at Glasshoughton Colliery near Pontefract.

Several years ago, Glasshoughton employed an attendant to issue tools to the workforce as and when they were required. At the beginning of one particular shift, the tool attendant was approached by a stranger in overalls, who had a large scar down one side of his face. The attendant greeted him and, as he did not recognise him and assumed that he must be new to the colliery, asked his name. The stranger replied 'Pete'. The attendant turned to get the tools he required, but when he turned back, Pete had disappeared. He never returned, and after the shift had finished the attendant brought this to the attention of a colleague who had worked at Glasshoughton for many years.

This colleague insisted that there was nobody known as Pete currently on the workforce, and when asked to describe the man, the attendant noted that the most distinguishing feature was the scar on his face. At this, his colleague appeared stunned, explaining that he had once known a Glasshoughton collier named Pete, who had a large scar down one side of his face... but Pete had been dead for many years.

Grimethorpe Colliery

The occasional appearance of a gentleman wearing a grey suit, with no helmet or lamp and seemingly not connected with the colliery at all, startled several miners working underground at Grimethorpe in Barnsley. Rumours of the inexplicable figure soon spread throughout the workforce, who nicknamed him 'Charlie'. Although at first thought to be a hoax, the sightings continued until certain colliers refused to visit the seam where he had been seen alone. No clue to his identity was ever forthcoming, and Charlie remained a mystery... or perhaps a hoax planned by one of the workforce!

A more specific, but unconnected sighting, from 1978, is reported by a former Grimethorpe miner, Jim (whose full name has been withheld on request.) As an engineer, Jim often worked alone on haulage engines in an isolated area of the pit. On one particular night shift, he was joined by a man he didn't recognise, whom he assumed had been drafted in from another colliery.

The stranger introduced himself as 'Joe', they chatted together, and worked for a while until a message came over the tannoy for Jim to stop the haulage and leave the site. When the deputy informed him that the belt needed shunting, Jim replied that Joe, who was still on site, could operate it without the need for him to return. The deputy had no record of anybody else in that area of the pit, and pointed out that, if a man had entered or left, his only route would have been to pass them directly, which nobody had.

Two deputies and three staff immediately went to the haulage area, and found it empty. However, a shovel and a half-cleared pile of coal were in place where Jim had last seen Joe working. Jim had spent enough time with the mystery miner to give a good description, and he had also been told his full name (also withheld here on request). On reporting this to control, it was confirmed that nobody of this name was underground. However, from the description given by Jim, the mystery miner was identified shortly afterwards by a colleague who had worked with him over thirty years before ... until his death in the 1940's.

Interestingly enough, in this case, rather than disbelieving Jim's story, pit officials asked him to keep quiet about it, so that men did not refuse to work in this area of the pit. The immediate family of the ghostly miner soon heard of the sighting, and approached Jim themselves. He gave them the same description of "Joe" and they, too, confirmed that

Jim had indeed seemingly talked to a relative of theirs, the ghost of a man he had never met!

The Lantern Boy, Conisbrough

The Doncaster district has records of coal mining dating back several hundred years, so it comes as no surprise that one of Conisbrough's best-known spectres has been wandering the landscape for over a century!

In times of old, children were employed underground to act as 'trappers', opening and closing wooden trap-doors to aid air circulation in the tunnels for the miners below ground. Their wages were poor and hours were long. At the beginning of each shift they would be issued with a small piece of candle, and when this burned itself out, the children continued working in darkness. A spectre commonly known as the Lantern Boy was believed to be the spirit of such a trapper, who had died in a tragic accident underground at a Doncaster colliery in the 1800's.

Until the middle of this century, sightings of the Lantern Boy were quite commonplace in and around isolated areas of Conisbrough. The ghost was last seen around 1945 by a young man who was walking near the crags between Conisbrough and Denaby, close to the site of a cemetery. He described the spirit as a 'pit trapper' in appearance, carrying a bright light and wearing tattered clothes. However, the most unusual thing about this child was that the young man was able to see straight through him! As no sightings of the Lantern Boy have been recorded recently, whether or not he still walks the lonely hills in Conisbrough is unknown.

Houghton Main Colliery

On 30th December 1886, ten miners climbed into the transport cage of Houghton Main Colliery in Barnsley, to travel to the pit bottom and start their shift. The winding engine was activated, and the cage began to move - and hurtled over five hundred yards down into the Barnsley coal seam, out of control. The ten miners never saw the beginning of their shift; they were killed instantly with the force of impact at the floor of the lift shaft. The winding engine man, responsible for lowering the cage, was tried for manslaughter but later acquitted. Although mining safety had improved drastically since earlier in the century, standards were not as stringent as they were to become later, impelled by the number of accidents like this.

Such tragic accidents were not without repercussions - in the late 1800's there were still colliers who believed in leaving gifts of coal and food to appease 'mine spirits', and so many unexpected deaths in the colliery must doubtless have encouraged even the least fertile imagination to believe that Houghton was jinxed... and later haunted. It has been said that mysterious cries were heard in the depths of the underground workings for a long time after the accident, and that the source of these was never traced.

Kellingley Colliery

Level Seventeen of this West Yorkshire colliery was long believed to be haunted, although nobody ever identified the ghost. The following tale was recounted by a colleague of the man it involved.

In the mid-1980's, three miners were underground towards the end of a shift, one of them being on Level Seventeen on his own. This gentleman noticed a stranger sitting in a particular gate, and although he was not aware that any extra staff were underground at that time, he approached him for a chat. For almost half an hour the pair were engaged in conversation, when it came to the end of the shift and the first miner left to get transport back to the pit top. Noticing that only himself and two colleagues were present, he asked the operator to wait for the fourth man who was still on Level Seventeen. He was assured that nobody else was underground, only the three of them. The following day, the frightened man did not return to work!

Wheldale Colliery

Colliers from Wheldale, in West Yorkshire, claimed that they had seen an unknown miner approach the airdoors which separated Wheldale from its neighbouring pit via a single, long tunnel. The airdoors had been installed for ventilation purposes, and miners from these collieries rarely crossed into each other's workings, certainly not without authorisation. Naturally, colleagues shouted the man back, although he appeared not to hear and carried on walking, through the airdoors and into the tunnel. Concerned that authorisation had not been given, and the collier had not responded to instructions to go no further, management telephoned the neighbouring colliery immediately. Staff at the other end of the tunnel waited for the man's appearance at their end. Nobody came out of the other side. Knowing that there were no further tunnels which branched off the main linking road, the solution seemed obvious: the miner (whose identity had still not been established) must be still inside the tunnel, and had to be fetched out.

The two collieries assessed the situation and agreed that one manager from each pit must enter the tunnel, so as to give the miner no chance of remaining undiscovered. Amid much speculation, the men began their journey, from different ends of the tunnel... and met in the middle, having seen and heard nothing. They scoured the area thoroughly, but nobody was in sight. By now the deputies were extremely concerned and it was decided to account for each and every man on the Wheldale Colliery side, to reveal the identity of the man. But when they did so, nobody was missing. A similar search on the other side of the tunnel gave the same results, and the mystery was never conclusively solved.

Thornhill Colliery

When an airdoor was installed at Thornhill Colliery, miners who were in the vicinity were often surprised to hear what sounded like heavy footsteps passing overhead. They looked for numerous solutions as to the cause of the noises, but remained unsure. Many of the miners who had heard the sound likened it to a group of people wearing wooden clogs, walking on the 'ceiling' above them. Some time later it was discovered that the site of the new airdoor was directly underneath a very old roadway, which would once have been on one of the earliest workings in the colliery. Early colliers in heavy wooden-soled workboots would have walked this way at the beginning and end of every shift. Is it possible that the modern colliers could have heard noises from the past?

Creswell Colliery

This North Nottinghamshire colliery has its own interesting folk tale, which dates back to the early 1900's. A miner walking home after his shift is said to have courted a Creswell woman, whose husband had conveniently just left her to commence his own shift down the mine. After his illicit visit, the miner left his love to walk home to Clowne via Markland Craggs. Atop of the Craggs, silhouetted by the full moon, he espied the Devil himself. Somehow Old Nick knew of the man's philandering, cursed him and sent him on his way. The miner arrived home to his own wife at dawn, white-haired and talking gibberish... and was 'of no use to man or beast thereafter'!

Stories of miners encountering the prince of darkness have been recorded elsewhere in the country. The Durham folk song *Collier's Rant* - often performed at Miners' Galas - carries the famous lines

> "As me and me marra (mate) was gannin' ti wark
> We met wi' the De'il, it was in the dark ..."

According to Ed Law, who recounted the Creswell tale, it was used as a threat by a particularly large local lady with whom he was acquainted, who suspected that her small, timid husband had a wandering eye. Apparently she had heard a similar tale as a child in Clowne in the 1920's, and repeated her own version at regular intervals as a warning to her poor husband!

South Kirby Colliery

Barnsley miner Glenn Washington recounted the following story, concerning an experience which a colleague had in the early 1980's. This man was a maintenance engineer at South Kirby Colliery, and was performing the routine duty of walking along the belt line, ensuring that it was in working order as it transported coal. He noticed a figure in the distance, removing spillage with a shovel and throwing it back on to the belt. The engineer did not recognise the man, although they exchanged names and stopped for a chat before he continued along the belt. It was over an hour later when a deputy was made aware that another miner was working in the area. Convinced that nobody should have been there, he contacted control, giving the name which the stranger had given to the maintenance engineer - only to receive the reply that a man of this name had died twenty years previously! Needless to say, when they rushed back to the belt, there was nobody in sight.

Rational Explanations?

Although it would not be conceivable to try to explain away every 'supernatural' happening associated with mining, there are certainly rational explanations for some events. For example, phantom miners' lamps have always been a favourite underground tale, used to frighten new recruits in particular, and West Yorkshire ex-miner Matt Kitchen gave a plausible explanation for such sightings.

Mr Kitchen noted that on several occasions, young miners fixing machine belts underground would report the appearance of a mysterious light in the distance. Repair work was carried out in isolated areas of the mines, which were often very quiet, and this in itself could have heightened the responses of many a nervous apprentice. There have been frequent reports from many collieries that a mysterious miner's lamp has been spotted half-way down a gate, which then disappears when the collier who spotted it turns his own lamp off. Mr Kitchen had experienced this himself, but pointed out that an abundance of metal tins, which carried spare parts for the repair of machine belts, were littered around in the workings. Lamplight would strike these at a certain angle and reflect off them; when the miner turned his own light out, the 'phantom light' would also disappear. Needless to say, when spare parts began to be packed in cardboard boxes instead of metal tins, the stories of ghostly lights reduced dramatically!

Wizard riding on back of giant cat.

19

The mysterious Padfoot beast: dog or giant cat, friend or deadly foe?

The Padfoot Legend

The age-old legend of the Padfoot is common throughout the British Isles, and superstition traditionally tells how the sighting of this large black hound foreshadows death and disaster. Throughout the centuries, the Padfoot has been recorded both as a sign of ill-omen and also as a protective guardian of lone travellers on secluded trails. Although in modern times the belief in such a creature is not as strong as it once was, there are still those who can tell their own stories of the appearance of mysterious 'spirit' dogs.

The Black Dog of Death

A Rotherham woman who wishes to be known only as Emma contributed the following tale, which bears witness to the legend that death is often foretold by the sighting a black Padfoot.

Emma was a geriatric nurse all her working life, and has cared for literally hundreds of dying patients. Many of the older nurses with whom she came into contact, throughout her career in various South Yorkshire hospitals, had the firm belief that patients close to death were often visited by a ghostly black hound in their final hours, which came to take them from this life into the next. Emma was quick to point out that she herself had never witnessed this, although she did not disbelieve their stories. In fact, it was not until she nursed her sick brother Roy through his final weeks that she had first-hand experience of the Padfoot legend.

One fine summer day shortly before Roy died, he and Emma were sitting in the back garden enjoying the sunshine. Roy grumbled that yet again he had to use the bathroom, and stood up to make the short trip through the garden and into the house. A few moments later he reappeared, smiling and telling Emma that 'the most beautiful black dog' had walked beside him as he made his way inside, before disappearing without a trace. Rather than being frightened or mystified by the experience, Roy was intrigued, and described the sighting of the hound with pleasure. Shortly afterwards, he died. Emma remains convinced that the stories she heard from the older nurses on her wards were true... and that the phantom Padfoot does indeed herald death.

The Hillsborough Padfoot

Yorkshire is riddled with age-old tales of the mythical ghostly dog which is often said to appear alongside travellers in isolated places. Perhaps its presence in the following story was a protective measure for the man who encountered it, as he travelled alone through a deserted area...

One winter's night in the late 1960's, a young policeman, Mr J K Ford, was on late foot patrol duty in the Hillsborough area of Sheffield. The night was cold and still, and when all his routine property checks were completed, at around midnight, snow began to fall. It settled instantly and soon became a blizzard, so PC Ford took shelter in a shop doorway to wait for the worst to pass. The streets were quiet as there was very little nightlife in this area, and traffic was non-existent due to the bad weather.

At 2.30 in the morning, PC Ford was still waiting for the snow to stop - by now there were four inches on the ground. It was at this point that he noticed a very large dog, which appeared to be a cross between a greyhound and an Irish wolf hound, running down the centre of the road. It passed the sheltering man without a glance, travelling at great speed, and panting loudly. The dog came from the direction of Dykes Hall Road and disappeared onto Taplin Road. Whether it was boredom or curiosity which made him decide to follow, PC Ford is not sure, but he came out of the shelter of the shop doorway and ran after the dog. Its tracks were clearly imprinted in the snow, enabling him to follow, and he rounded the corner onto Taplin Road after it. There was no sight of the strange hound. This did not surprise PC Ford, as he recalled that it had been travelling at a good speed. Still following the tracks, he traced the route of the animal as it appeared to have crossed the road close to a garage... then the tracks stopped dead.

In the middle of an empty road, with nowhere the dog could have leapt to or hidden, the paw prints came to an abrupt halt. The policeman searched the immediate area in an attempt to come up with a satisfactory explanation as to how the animal could possibly have disappeared without trace. He never found one.

The Bowshaw Padfoot

Bowshaw House is an historic Georgian building near Dronfield with a colourful and mysterious past, which is described in more detail in a later chapter. Jean and Keith Rowlinson, who have lived there for nearly twenty years, have a wealth of ghostly stories to tell, although one of their more unusual tales concerns a spectral hound which has been heard and felt on several occasions, but never actually seen!

The Rowlinsons had been living at Bowshaw for around two years when Jean first experienced something unusual. She was kneeling at the fireplace one afternoon building up a fire, when she heard the pattering of paws on the carpet behind her. At the time, she owned a dog called Bess and assumed that it must have wandered into the room. Then, when Jean felt a gentle shove on her back, she turned around to tell Bess to stop it... only to find that the room was empty!

Jean's mother Joyce Naylor lived at Bowshaw Lodge, which adjoins Bowshaw House at one end, during the 1980s. Every Friday evening Joyce would bake, and one autumn evening at around 9.30pm, she was in the kitchen alone, her husband having gone out for a drink. Joyce bent down to pick up a baking-tray from a cupboard, and felt a gentle push on her back from behind. She turned sharply to see nothing there, although she felt at the time that a dog rather than a human had been responsible. When the lodge was eventually sold off as a property in its own right, its next tenant, a man named Michael, called in on Joyce one day to ask whether she had ever had a strange sensation in the kitchen area of the house ... that of being pushed gently! He, too, described a similar experience to Joyce and her daughter Jean, although nobody can guess at the identity of the phantom hound.

The Aston Panther

Over the last twenty or so years, tales of sightings of large, mysterious black cats have taken their place in contemporary folklore, and have grown into a modern legend which rivals that of the age-old Yorkshire belief in the Padfoot. From the Beast of Exmoor to more locally-based South Yorkshire sightings, including those on the moors at Penistone, the legend grows with each telling, and the areas of Swallownest, Todwick and Aston are not without their claims to possessing an elusive black creature similar in appearance to a panther.

Steve Moore, a Dinnington man in his late twenties, caught sight of such a beast when walking home with a friend very early one morning in 1991. It was the middle of June and the pair had been to watch a late film at the Crystal Peaks cinema. The dawn was just beginning to break as they walked beside the dual carriageway from Beighton towards Dinnington. They had reached the Aston/Swallownest junctions when a large black creature darted from the left hand side of the road, around 150 yards in front of them, and quickly disappeared into trees to their right. The animal appeared and vanished so quickly that Mr Moore's companion did not catch sight of it, but he himself remains convinced that it was too large to be an ordinary cat, and yet certainly not a dog! Several other locals of this area have testified to having seen the same creature, although it has eluded capture and, so far, nobody has successfully caught it on film...

An early woodcut of a werewolf attack: but how many were really Padfoot encounters, rather than victims of Lycanthropy?

Poltergeists

Poltergeist activity is often the most frightening kind of haunting to experience, during which objects are thrown around and can appear and disappear without warning, strange noises are heard, and occupants of the house can be directly hurt by an unseen malevolent force. Exorcisms have no guarantee of success, and some such hauntings can carry on for years before stopping suddenly of their own accord. The following two stories are accounts of hauntings which could very possibly be considered cases of poltergeist activity.

The Rotherham Poltergeist

The following story was recounted by a lady who would rather that her family remained anonymous, so pseudonyms will be employed in what follows. As the focus for this story is a council house in the Rotherham area which is currently occupied, no address can be given.

In 1983, Mrs Sheila Davis invited her daughter Kim Taylor, with her husband Scott and their little girl Kelly, to lodge with her until they had found a suitable council house. As only three choices of council accommodation are given, the Taylors were forced to take up one of these offers or lose their place on the waiting list. Having chosen a house close to Mrs Davis, the responsibility for minding baby Kelly alternated between Mrs Davis and Scott, as Kim worked shifts.

The house needed redecorating throughout, so Mrs Davis offered to do it herself, and spent an initial day preparing wallpaper to save time the following day. She laid strips over the pasting tables in each room, so that the next day they would all be in order for her to begin work. On her return, however, the wallpapers were mixed up, and no longer remained in the rooms in which they were originally laid. Suspecting that somebody had somehow entered the house during the night, Mrs Davis checked the doors and windows but found them secure.

The Wonders of the Invisible World.

OBSERVATIONS

As well *Historical* as *Theological*, upon the NATURE, the NUMBER, and the OPERATIONS of the

DEVILS.

Accompany'd with,

I. Some Accounts of the Grievous Molestations, by DÆ-MONS and WITCHCRAFTS, which have lately annoy'd the Countrey; and the Trials of some eminent *Malefactors* Executed upon occasion thereof: with several Remarkable *Curiosities* therein occurring.

II. Some Counsils, Directing a due Improvement of the terrible things, lately done, by the Unusual & Amazing Range of EVIL SPIRITS, in Our Neighbourhood: & the methods to prevent the *Wrongs* which those *Evil Angels* may intend against all sorts of people among us. especially in Accusations of the Innocent.

III. Some Conjectures upon the great EVENTS, likely to befall, the WORLD in General, and NEW EN-GLAND in Particular; as also upon the Advances of the TIME, when we shall see BETTER DAYES.

IV. A short Narrative of a late Outrage committed by a knot of WITCHES in *Swedeland*, very much Resembling, and so far Explaining, *That* under which our parts of *America* have laboured!

V. THE DEVIL DISCOVERED: In a Brief Discourse upon those TEMPTATIONS, which are the more Ordinary *Devices* of the Wicked One.

By Cotton Mather.

Boston Printed by *Benj. Harris* for *Sam. Phillips*. 1693.

Cases of 'possession' and possible Poltergeist phenomena were often attributed to Witchcraft

During the following week, decorating implements which had been put in a storage cupboard disappeared without trace, and curtain tracks left in the house overnight were moved into different rooms. Not wanting to alarm her daughter and son-in-law, Mrs Davis decided on a policy of silence. Although she was convinced that nobody could have entered the house, especially not just to move things around for fun, she was loath to look for a supernatural explanation. Even though the atmosphere in the house was somehow 'inhospitable', feeling rather cold and damp, Mrs Davis preferred to think that this was due to the fact that it had remained unoccupied for nine months previously.

Kim and Scott Taylor moved into the house, unaware of the problems which had been experienced by Kim's mother. Underneath the stairs was a small recess where the dog's basket was placed, although the dog always seemed reluctant to settle there. At first it was felt that the animal was simply disobedient, although on one occasion when Mrs Davis was called on to babysit her granddaughter, she realised that the explanation was not so simple. This particular day, the dog was howling and scratching to be let out into the garden. Once outside, it continued to howl in a way which Mrs Davis felt to be unnatural. She watched the animal, which seemed so distressed that she let it back into the kitchen again. Once inside, it continued to yelp and scratch at the door to go out.

Concerned, Mrs Davis opened the door again, and the dog ran out again into the centre of the garden. She watched in horror as it slowly rose off all fours into mid-air as though it was being lifted, and then seemed to be hurled through the air at the closed kitchen door, hitting it with some force and banging loudly before falling to the ground. The dog yelped and ran back into the garden, reaching the centre before being raised slowly into the air again. Mrs Davis watched as it flew towards the kitchen door for a second time, hitting it with another thud. It picked itself up with a yelp and ran out of the garden, disappearing from sight. Mrs Davis, still unaware whether her daughter and son-in-law had experienced any strange happenings in the house at all, simply told them on their return that the dog had run away. The family never saw their pet again.

When Kim and Scott decided to separate later that same year, Mrs Davis took their daughter Kelly to live at their house. Kim remained in the house alone for a while. Mrs David and her husband were keen for Kelly to be reunited with her mother, although each time the little girl visited the house she would scream to leave. It was around this time that Mrs Davis became aware that a Ouija board had been used in the house at some point. Although it cannot conclusively be proved that this precipitated strange happenings in the house, the Ouija board is notoriously dangerous as a method of communication with the spirit world and is often associated with poltergeist cases.

The first Mrs Davis knew of her daughter experiencing strange happenings in the house was around this time. A box of matches placed on the arm of a chair by Kim disappeared without trace; a thorough search under chairs and in drawers did not reveal it. The box was later found in the ash pan of the coal fire, unburned. The fire had gone out one night and filled the room with smoke without reason, and Mrs Davis had insisted on having the chimney swept to see whether a cause could be found. Although there was no logical reason, the box of matches was unearthed to the amazement of Kim, who knew that they could not possibly have been there!

From then on, Kim began to tell her mother more stories of strange goings-on in the house. From a small cupboard in Kelly's bedroom which was used to store toys strange noises would issue, as though a child was playing with rattles and things within it. Kim searched for whatever was causing the sounds, although they always stopped whenever she opened the cupboard door. In the end, she resorted to leaving it permanently open in an attempt to stop whatever it was.

Two years had elapsed since Mrs Davis had initially looked after her granddaughter, and by now Kim had remarried. For a while everything in the house remained quiet, although she and her new husband soon began to be continually bothered by the sounds of a roller-skating child, which would begin usually as soon as they had put Kelly to bed. Concerned that their daughter would be woken, the couple took it in turns to check the alleyway next to the house, where the noise appeared to be reverberating against the wall. Nobody was ever there, and as soon as they left the house the noise stopped. This went on for at least two days, until Kim's husband ran out to catch the offender - and could still hear the skates, but found no children playing anywhere in the vicinity of the house. When they eventually retired to bed that night, the sound of roller-skates began again... but rather than sounding as though they were outside, the couple realised that the noise was coming from their own middle bedroom! They made their way to the door and opened it sharply, but all was suddenly still and quiet inside.

The couple had always felt that the living room was not a pleasant place to stay, since a cold draught would pick up and circle round their feet whenever they settled there. Kim and her husband were about to go to bed one evening when they became aware that the atmosphere in the living room had suddenly become 'hostile'. Smoke began to pour from the coke fire into the room, and as it did so, a male voice which was familiar to Kim seemed to float from the fireplace, with the smoke, uttering a name over and over again. Two years previously, a friend of Kim's had died in a tragic motorbike accident, and yet it seemed to be his voice, and his name, which were echoing around the room. The voice rapidly became a scream, and further sounds made it appear as though the moment of the crash was being relived. The couple were so terrified that they hastily dressed and left, running all the way to Brinsworth to spend the night with relatives rather than sleeping at home.

The source of the noises was never found, and as Kim and her husband were by now expecting another child, they were forced to return to their council house soon afterwards. Mrs Davis, in preparation for the arrival of her second grand-child, had begun to collect baby-gro's and other clothes and baby toys for Kim. Kim saved all such gifts in her airing cupboard, and made a considerable collection in the few weeks before the baby was born. However, the day Kim was admitted to hospital, she searched the airing cupboard and found it empty. It crossed her mother's mind that Kim might have given away some of the gifts because she did not like them, but this was not the case. Their next assumption was that Kelly had somehow removed the baby's things in childish jealousy, although in actual fact there was no way that a child so young could possibly have reached the high shelf in the airing cupboard where they were stored. The missing baby things were never found.

After arrival of the baby, everything remained quiet in the house for a while. Several months elapsed before Kim and her husband encountered a new problem. Kim's eldest daughter Kelly was now six years old, and had begun to suffer from what Kim described as 'mood swings'. She appeared silent and self-absorbed, in contrast to her former cheerful self. One evening Kelly was sitting crayoning in the living room, with her mother close by. Kim noticed the door to the stairs beginning to open slowly, and a white cloud of smoke-like substance seemed to form in the open doorway. Kelly stopped drawing and appeared entranced, stood up slowly, and walked into the cloud of shapeless mist. She wandered through it and sat on the bottom stair. The vapour appeared to follow the little girl and rest around her as she sat expressionless and entranced. Kim could hardly believe what she had seen, and although she tried to rationalise the situation, she felt that if her daughter was sleepwalking it would be wise not to panic and try and rouse her. Her attempts to speak gently to her daughter were unsuccessful, as she seemed deeply entranced. It was only after the mist-like substance had disappeared and Kelly had come round that Kim was able to ask her more. Kelly said that 'Julie' had come to play with her, and described her as a girl a little older than herself. From here onwards, this whole scenario became a regular occurrence, and always around the same time in the evening, just before Kelly's bed time. On no occasion did any other member of the family report seeing anything more detailed than a cloud of mist-like substance, and when pressed further about her invisible friend, Kelly would merely point to the door to the stairs where Julie appeared from.

Mrs Davis tried to reassure her daughter that Kelly most likely had an imaginary friend, in common with most children, although considering this alongside the other unusual occurrences in the house made both women worry that there was far more to the situation than that. As time went on, they tried to get more information about Julie's visits from Kelly. The little girl explained that Julie lived in the house, and was eight years old. For a while the situation continued with no developments; as Kelly got older, she described Julie as getting older - until eventually Julie appeared to become hostile.

Kelly would wake in the middle of the night screaming that Julie had hit her or bitten her. In an attempt to reassure her daughter, Kim would tuck Kelly into bed at night and stay with the little girl until she drifted off to sleep. On one such occasion, she had just left the bedroom and had reached the top of the stairs when a crash and a scream made her run back in to find Kelly at the other side of the bedroom, as though she had been hurled out of bed and half way across the room. It was this final incident which prompted Kim and her mother to confide in each other the many things which had happened in the house over the years, which they had tried for the most part to keep to themselves.

Shortly after this, they decided to seek further advice on exorcising the house, since the sudden aggression which the presence exhibited was becoming potentially dangerous to the two children. After a number of unsuccessful enquiries Mrs Davis made concerning exorcism, she finally approached a Church of England clergyman with experience in this type of problem, who offered to help. The vicar asked the family relevant questions about the type of activity in the house, and paid them a visit confirming that he too could feel a very strong presence within. Then, he spent several days completing his own research connected with the area on which the house was built. When he contacted the family again, it was to confirm that a young girl called Julie, who had died at the age of eight years old, had lived in a house which had occupied the site of Kim's current home, before the council estate had been built. Julie was one of three children, and was buried in the local churchyard. It was generally felt that the area at the bottom of the stairs where the presence had been manifesting itself was the very spot on which the child Julie had died many years before.

When a date for the exorcism was set, the family were warned not to discuss the forthcoming event inside the house at all, but just to carry on as though everything were normal. Julie was not to be mentioned by name, and neither were any of the strange happenings in the house to be talked about. The children were removed to safety, and when the vicar and his associates arrived at the house they sat in the lounge along with the family, in total silence. Beginning with the lounge and leaving Kelly's bedroom until last of all, the vicar and his team performed the necessary rituals throughout every room.

In Kelly's bedroom, the group were silent both before and after the ritual, taking longer here as it was felt to be the centre of the activity. On completion of the ritual, a terrible smell, which Kim and her husband likened to the 'smell of death' and burned charcoal, filled the house. The temperature briefly plummeted to freezing coldness, until the group

31

returned downstairs to sit in meditation for a while. The atmosphere changed to one of peace almost instantly, and the vicar and his colleagues left a short while later.

The family could not believe the difference to the atmosphere of the house which the exorcism ritual made, and subsequently had no more trouble; the building was filled with an atmosphere of peace which it had never before possessed.

The Swallownest Poltergeist

The couple who recounted the following story have requested that their names be changed, and that the address of their former home is not revealed in full, since poltergeist activity succeeded in driving them out of their house in Swallownest several years ago, after only a relatively short stay.

John and Alison Watts moved into an old house on Alexandra Road in the early 1980's. Although they were later told by their neighbours that the house had been boarded up for many years prior to their buying it, this did not concern the Watts, and they never felt curious enough to look into the history of the building.

The first thing the family noticed on moving in was that the house proved difficult to heat, the upstairs rooms being particularly cold, the worst of which was the bathroom. The Watts had not been in residence for long when they began to hear strange noises in the night, which would wake them regularly, although they had no idea of the cause. Rationally, they put these down to the creaks and bangs which were normal in such an old house. However, within a few weeks of moving in, Mr and Mrs Watts also noticed that certain personal belongings were disappearing - they were always small objects which would have been easy to mislay, such as car keys and other small but vital possessions. On one occasion a set of keys which had been missing for several weeks finally turned up in an unused sideboard drawer.

Despite their mounting suspicions, the couple remained sceptical and insisted that they 'did not believe in ghosts'. Then certain 'phantom' smells began, namely that of pipesmoke which appeared on the landing, and continued to do so throughout the Watts' three-year stay in the house. One afternoon when Mrs Watts went into the bathroom, a strange mist gathered in front of her eyes, and then, in a flash, it was gone. The couple by now decided that the atmosphere in the bathroom was particularly sinister.

Inexplicable shadows could often be seen in two corners of the living room, and a video recorder which was kept in one of these corners had the habit of re-setting itself onto a blank channel in the middle of recording a programme. The Watts noted that they seemed to get through an enormous quantity of light bulbs; the number which exploded prematurely went far beyond mere coincidence. When for the second time a set of car keys went missing, Mrs Watts paid to have another set recut, before they fell out of her coat pocket six weeks later as she bent down to put it in the washing machine. She had worn the coat every day since the keys went missing, and her pockets were the first place she had checked!

One evening Mr Watts was fixing a pair of stereo speakers to the living room wall when he noticed that the loose ends of wire appeared to have a life of their own... and called his wife into the room where they stood in fascination watching the wire ends dance and jig on their own. A similar thing happened with a houseplant shortly afterwards: the Watts sat up watching its leaves twitching and waving until 3 o'clock in the morning, although it was not in the presence of any draught which could explain its movement.

Mrs Watts often brought home paperwork to finish, and on one such occasion was sitting in the living room with an ashtray close to her chair. She had been engrossed for a while and had smoked several cigarettes, when she moved to fetch a ruler. When she sat down again, she glanced into the ashtray and noticed that her cigarette ends had been neatly arranged on top of a bed of pot pourri and a layer of ash. Only a short while later, the Watts were sharing a box of chocolates. Mrs Watts took two out each for her and her husband, and replaced the box in the fridge. When her husband commented on how greedy she was, Mrs Watts followed the direction of his gaze and saw a further three chocolates stacked neatly on the coffee table, which she most certainly had not taken out of the box!

Throughout their three years at the house on Alexandra Road, the Watts catalogued literally hundreds of strange experiences. All of the sightings except for one were restricted to the couple alone, and it was when their little granddaughter became involved that they finally became convinced that they would have to put their scepticism aside.

The Watts' granddaughter was three years old, and had been put to bed in the spare room early one evening. At around two o'clock in the morning, the couple were awakened by the sounds of the little girl talking to somebody. They entered the bedroom to find her sitting up in bed, far from sleepy and certainly not dreaming. The girl told them that she had been playing with a big black dog, which had appeared in the bedroom wanting to jump up at her. Although there was no sign of anything, the couple were so sure that their granddaughter was not dreaming that this proved to be the final straw as far as remaining in the house was concerned. Soon afterwards, it was put up for sale.

The Unexplained

While hauntings and things which go bump in the night would seem common-place in and around South Yorkshire, there are other tales of strange happenings which span time and defy all logical explanation. Ancient sites imbued with strange and powerful auras, visitors from beyond the grave who have messages for the living, and 'cursed' paintings which are found undamaged after inexplicable house fires, to name but a few. The following chapter explores a selection of unexplained mysteries from the South Yorkshire region.

Stocksbridge and the Dragon Legend

The Stocksbridge bypass has received such wide coverage in recent years that it is now considered to be one of the most haunted spots in the North, if not in the country. Stories of ghostly monks, unidentified shadows, strange noises and phantom children in period costume have dominated newspaper reports since its ill-fated opening, on Friday 13th in 1988. More recently, an episode of the television series *Strange But True* attempted to reconstruct some of the happenings which have dogged the site... which led to an influx of ghost-hunters flocking there armed with cameras, hoping for their own glimpse of the paranormal.

Wharncliffe Crags, the dark and foreboding rise of rock on Hunshelf Moor, close to the Stocksbridge bypass, is the focus for legends aplenty; the dragon of Wantley once reputedly used the site as his lair before being slain by a local lord, and has left his namesake in the form of the Dragon's Den cave. Dragon legends are common throughout England, surviving in place names and folk tales - not least of all in the immortal story of St George, the patron saint of England. The image of the dragon possibly came to symbolise the old pagan powers which were usurped when Christianity became the dominant religion, around 600 AD. It

St George the Dragon Slayer, depicted beside the corpse of one such unfortunate beast. The story of 'More of More Hall' and the Wantley Dragon is similar to that of St George.

therefore comes as no surprise to find that Christian saints were the slayers of dragons.

In earlier cultures, the dragon was seen as the guardian of buried treasure, as characterised by Tolkien's cave-dwelling dragon Smaug in *The Hobbit*. Today, both the dragons and their 'treasure' (which could represent ancient sites of earth power rather than hoards of gold) remain hidden, only revealing their fabled haunts via the folk-memory of place-names and legends. The image of the dragon-slayer himself has changed throughout history to incorporate the more ordinary lord of the manor who, like 'More of More Hall' in the case of the Wantley dragon at Stocksbridge, sought to rescue the land from the ravages of the great beast. The dragon connection with the Stocksbridge area suggests that it was a place of fable and supernatural legend hundreds of years before 20th century folk began to report their strange sightings here.

Stocksbridge and its Haunted History

The area around Stocksbridge is riddled with tales of supernatural disturbances, not being confined to the infamous 'ghost bridge' alone. Rumours of ghostly soldiers on Tankersley Moor abound, where an old battle site is said to have witnessed the deaths of many men. An early copper mine in the Stocksbridge area hosted a disaster said to have killed several children earlier this century, and their spirits have reputedly found no rest in death. Alongside these, the infamous dark hooded figure of a monk not only walks the bypass, but has been spotted travelling along some of the lonelier country lanes which run over Hunshelf Moor.

In 1959, the Dowager Countess of Wharncliffe, from a family connected with the area for many generations, confessed to being plagued by numerous spirit presences at her family seat, the 18th century Carlton House in Wortley. She also spotted the ghost of the first Lord Wharncliffe, who died in the 1700's, near to the old Georgian Wharncliffe family home of of Wortley Hall. Shortly afterwards, the Countess requested that a local priest come to bless every room in her house, as the spirits were getting increasingly mischievous.

The nearby Sheffield district of Oughtibridge (thought by some to translate from the Anglo-Saxon for 'Demon's Bridge') made regional news in 1992 when plans for building a new housing estate threatened to disturb the site of a 16th century burial-ground. A local of the area commented at the time: 'I wouldn't like to be an unsuspecting homebuyer trying to raise babies on a plague graveyard only to find children sicken and grow weaker for no apparent reason. Older villagers are positive about the area's history and it is a very strange place. It is often shrouded in fog when the rest of the area is in brilliant sunshine...'

Several ghost-hunters have noted that ancient sites such as stone circles, old crags and ley lines are often the focus for paranormal activity. Other researchers feel that modern electricity pylons somehow act as a magnet for certain types of 'spirit activity'. Interestingly, the area around the Stocksbridge bypass possesses both - in the ancient site of the Dragon's Den and in the modern electricity pylons which run across the landscape. (As described later, a particularly unusual sighting occurred underneath the pylon next to the 'ghost bridge' itself.) If either of these theories is true, then perhaps it is with little surprise that Stocksbridge plays host to so many unusual presences.

The Black Monk and Other Sightings

Several serious accidents, of which eight have been fatal, have occurred since the opening of the bypass, prompting Hillsborough MP Helen Jackson to call for the area to be a marked accident blackspot less that five years after its opening. Although many accidents have been put down to bad road design and driver error, more and more people are coming forward to suggest that another altogether more sinister force is at work.

Rather than strange happenings having been prompted by the building of the bypass, as has often been suggested, it would seem that paranormal activity has been recorded in Stocksbridge throughout the century. One local woman reported seeing the spectre of a 'dark hooded figure' on the road to Wortley, before the bypass had been built, on a misty night in the early 1970's. And local woman Katina Hewitt described to *The Star* newspaper how her grandmother had seen the figure of a monk several times when her family lived in White Row Farm at Hunshelf. This means that the spectre was appearing regularly at least eighty years ago, long before the bypass had even been thought of. Local children were told that the monk was the ghost of a Catholic priest who had visited the area to take a secret Mass in one of the farm cottages. The priest supposedly lost a sacred relic as he travelled over the moors, and never returned from his search to find the artefact. Some versions of the tale suggest that the priest was killed by soldiers; others say that he died a mysterious death on the lonely moor, and that his body was never recovered.

More recent sightings of the phantom monk, by motorists and joggers alike, note that its appearance has been accompanied by a 'strange musty smell', which one person described as 'similar to an antique shop'. Another motorist and her companion noticed the over-powering smell of pipe smoke in their car as they drove through the area, despite neither of them smoking. In the early 1990's, a truck driver broke down close to the bridge, and on checking his engine, was astounded to find that the thick rubber engine belts had been removed (completely unbroken) causing the engine to seize! He struggled to replace them before restarting the vehicle, which was otherwise in good working order.

Donald Nutbrown worked on the construction of Stocksbridge by-pass in the middle to late 1980's, and still recalls vividly an experience which he and a labourer had while working on part of the bypass which runs through a solid belt of rock. It was around one o'clock in the afternoon, in the summer of 1986, when simultaneously the two men felt an uncanny chill and for some reason looked up towards their right, in the direction of a pine plantation. Around ten yards away, a huge black form, which Mr Nutbrown described as 'much bigger than a normal person - a big black monk without a face', was standing as though watching them. The men dropped their equipment and swiftly left the site. There was a belief among some of the site workers at the time that a Viking burial ground was located in the area, since the original plans for the bypass were to lay a total of four lanes. When these plans were vetoed and the reason was never made public, rumours spread quickly. Even today, Mr Nutbrown pointed out that most of the accidents on the bypass have occurred in the area where he and his colleague saw the black figure, near to the alleged site of the burial ground.

The story which brought mysterious events around Stocksbridge bypass into the public eye centred on happenings in the late 1980's. Before the bypass was even completed, security guards Steven Brookes and David Goldthorpe were on patrol one night when they caught sight of a group of children in period costume who appeared to be dancing in a ring around the electricity pylon near the top of the hill. The men turned their car to investigate further, although the children had vanished and no footprints were in evidence around the pylon. Local legend suggests that the appearance of phantom children often heralds misfortune for the beholder. Derbyshire psychic medium and author Wayne Anthony noted that some of these 'spectral children are referred to by ghost researchers as 'radiants' or 'invisibles', and could possibly be the souls of children who had died unfortunate deaths in the locality at an earlier period in history. Mr Boylan himself has researched several such stories, and notes that 'several of these spirits have been seen in the vicinity of former Derbyshire workhouses and mills.'

Puzzled, though not unduly frightened by their sighting, Mr Brookes and Mr Goldthorpe continued their surveillance until they spotted a figure on the unfinished bridge (which was inaccessible at the time). They later described it as 'dark and hooded' in outline, and noted that the headlights of their vehicle passed straight though it. But their most terrifying experience was yet to come: A huge luminous form appeared on the opposite side of the bridge and headed towards their car. Horrified, the two men immediately left the site and contacted their head of security, Mike Lee. It was 4.30 am, and Mr Lee was surprised to find both guards in severe shock. Mr Brookes and Mr Goldthorpe were so frightened that they approached a local vicar later that morning, requesting his assistance to exorcise the entity. Within weeks, both security guards had left their posts, unable to cope with the terror of whatever it was they had encountered in the small hours of that morning.

Although Mr Lee and a fellow manager visited the bypass soon afterwards to see for themselves what could be the root of the problem, their visit was without incident.

Research was undertaken into the area around the bypass, but no clues were forthcoming. Shortly afterwards, policeman Dick Ellis and John Beet were called out to investigate further, and parked their panda car at one end of the still incomplete bridge for a short spell of observation. They were about to leave after an uneventful hour when both men experienced a feeling of intense cold... and saw a figure clothed in dark costume with a white cravat, which appeared to be close to the side of the car. The figure disappeared in an instant. When the men left their car to investigate further, a loud bang was heard on the bodywork from the boot area, although nobody else was in the area and the cause of the noise remained unexplained. Thoroughly frightened, the policemen got back into the car and made several attempts to start the engine before they were finally able to leave.

Local psychic consultant Lucinda June Beevers was soon called in to investigate the strange happenings, and stories began to mount up after the initial publicity surrounding the case. As more people came forward and shared their stories, similar themes became noticeable, particularly concerning the spectre of the monk mentioned previously. Mrs Beevers herself experienced a dark and foreboding presence which appeared in her passenger seat as she drove over Stocksbridge bypass on one occasion. Despite being accustomed to psychic phenomena, she was aware of an intense sense of fear caused by the 'black shadow'.

Witches familiar

On a later occasion, Mrs Beevers spotted the same black shadow in the rear of another driver's car - although it disappeared as she overtook the vehicle. The sight or sense of something occupying a seat in a car which is supposedly empty would be enough to induce even the most hardened sceptic to lose control of a vehicle. Indeed, there are even reports of cars being turned completely around on this bleak and lonely stretch of road... by forces other than the driver.

A Visitor From Beyond the Grave

Shirley Marks was amazed when her sister told her that she had been 'visited' by their dead mother, a while after her death, in a vision in which she was holding out a small box which appeared to contain matches. Feeling that this was something of a warning, Shirley's sister instantly visited her widowed father, to find that he had accidentally set his flat alight the night before, after falling asleep with a lit cigarette in his hand. Although he had not been badly injured, when subsequently Shirley's sister had another vision, in which her mother was holding out a bottle of pills, she again feared for their father and rushed to his flat. This time she found that the old man had been up ill all night, and had been taking aspirin at regular intervals. After this, it became something of a family joke that if anything was ever wrong, Shirley's sister would have a visit from beyond the grave!

It came as a great surprise to Shirley when, several years after her mother's last reappearance to her sister, she appeared in a vision to her. Shirley was suffering a particularly disturbed night's sleep when she opened her eyes to see a white figure at the end of the bed. Although no face was visible, she found that she had her mother very strongly on her mind, and remembering that whenever a vision of their mother appeared to her sister it usually contained as message, telephoned her sister the next morning. Her brother-in-law had been rushed into hospital with a suspected heart attack. Around twelve months later, Shirley again had a restless night, and again awoke to find a vision of her mother, this time closer, and this time holding out her hand towards her, at the end of the bed. The following day she telephoned her sister to find that her husband had again been admitted to hospital with further heart trouble.

However, rather than these spirit visits continuing to be a source of solace, in 1993 Shirley reported an altogether different experience. She had arrived home late one evening after finishing her shift, and was watching television with her husband when something close to the living room window caught her eye - and within seconds a white mist (which only she could see) had almost entirely blotted everything else out of sight. In the distance, Shirley remembers being able to see something far away which appeared to be drawing closer through the mist, which eventually materialised as her mother, who had by now been dead for many years. All the while her limbs began to feel heavy and cold, and she was aware that her breathing had become unnaturally deep. Shirley was aware of her husband's voice in the distance pleading with her to 'wake up', and remembers sitting on her hands so that he could not move her. The vision of her mother appeared to be bathed in light which Shirley felt drawn towards, and yet she fought against this feeling, and eventually relaxed and fell into a deep sleep. When she awoke, her husband was bathing her forehead with a flannel, obviously shaken at her sudden and seemingly entranced state.

Shirley telephoned her sister the next day, but found nothing wrong. Some time later she returned home from work late again, and was watching television with her husband, much the same as before, when she was suddenly drawn to look at the exact spot in the living room where her previous vision had materialised. Her husband, who had always been sceptical about 'visits from beyond the grave', instantly recognised the signs and shouted to Shirley not to look. However, she had already felt her limbs becoming heavy, and a familiar chill overtook her. Shirley described how the white mist, in common with her first vision, began to spread and blot everything else out of sight, and again she saw her mother appear in the distance. She was aware of her husband shouting 'Leave us alone!' as the vision of her mother reached out her arms towards her, and described feeling as though her mother was somehow trying to 'enter' her body. Although outwardly Shirley appeared to be in a trance, with her husband frantically trying to wake her, she felt as though a struggle were going on inside herself to regain consciousness and keep her mother at a distance. In a short while the battle was over and Shirley lapsed into unconsciousness, the 'mist' receding and the vision disappearing completely.

Witches familiar

The following day, by now quite concerned, Shirley again telephoned her sister and described her experience of the previous night. Her sister was horrified, and advised her never to reach out her arms if the vision of their mother again appeared wanting to 'take her away'. At this point, both sisters remarked on the fact that their brother had died shortly after their mother; he had complained of a sore throat at her funeral, which had quickly developed into a tumour, and almost a year to the day after his mother's funeral, he too was dead.

Although on one occasion since, Shirley has felt her mother's presence - again when her husband was with her and was able to recognise the signs - this time her visit proved less traumatic. As she herself noted, it was almost as though some sort of battle had been won on the previous occasion, and this time the atmosphere quickly receded without her having slipped into a trance-state. The final words must go to Shirley's husband, who seems to have developed a certain resistance towards his wife's supernatural visitor. The last time he saw her eyes widen and look towards that certain spot by the living room window, he stood up and remarked: 'Oh no! If your mother's coming again I'd better go and get that kettle on...'

The Boiler Room

When Graham Bloodworth was made redundant from the toy department at Schofields, on Angel Street in Sheffield, he was offered alternative work as a security man in the same building. After the store had closed, he would lock every external door, and then lock the internal stairway doors after the cleaners had finished their shift. On his rounds at night, there was one particular area of the old building of which Mr

Bloodworth was wary, although at the time he had no idea why. This was the boiler room, located in the basement of the building. It was accessed by a large steel fire door, which was automatically closed by a pulley and weight system, and was always warm as it contained three large oil-fired boilers.

One evening Mr Bloodworth entered the boiler room, sliding the heavy fire door along its track, and being careful not to let it go as it had the habit of banging shut. He made his way across the room towards the fire escape on the other side, glancing to his left at the store room for Royal Doulton china, which was a locked door with a window that looked out into the boiler room. As Mr Bloodworth locked the fire door, he was aware of the hair on the back of his neck beginning to rise, and he started to feel decidedly uncomfortable. The temperature of the room dropped suddenly, his heart began to beat faster, and he described how 'there was a feeling of utter panic... it took me all my powers of reasoning to continue putting the Yale key in the lock to secure the door. As this feeling of dread increased, despite all the people (myself included) who say that ghosts cannot hurt you, I simply knew I had to get out of that room fast!'

The temperature of the boiler room had dropped to freezing coldness, and Mr Bloodworth had the distinct feeling that whatever was with him in the room was located in the Royal Doulton store. Running across the boiler room, he opened the heavy sliding door and dashed out onto the stairs, hitting the light switch on his way up. He ran so fast that he heard the boiler room fire door clang shut when he was already on his way up the second flight of steps! On arriving at the security lodge where his co-worker was sitting, Mr Bloodworth's white face must have spoken for him, because his colleague looked at him knowingly and said: 'You've seen it, then?'

Although Mr Bloodworth had actually seen nothing, just felt some-thing, he spoke to other staff in an attempt to find out what experiences other people had had in the boiler room. It emerged that nobody who worked on the Royal Doulton china department would venture down into the store room alone. One member of staff had once had a very similar experience to Mr Bloodworth's, feeling as though she were being watched, and had turned her head to see a glowing pair of feet hovering a foot off the floor! Theories about the haunted boiler room soon began to circulate the store. Several locals had heard rumours that a Quaker graveyard was once situated in this area which, disused and forgotten, had been built over. Whether this is in fact true nobody can say, but the haunting was not restricted to the boiler room alone: the store manager reported his office door opening and closing of its own accord quite frequently.

The Haunted Hall

Geriatric nurse Ian Woods remains a confirmed sceptic about the supernatural, despite having had several strange experiences throughout his career in various South Yorkshire nursing homes. One particular historic house which was recently converted into a residential home for the elderly, and is located on the South Yorkshire border, has been witness to a host of strange happenings.

A young female care assistant who started work at the Hall in the early 1990's never saw her first night out. She had gone to attend to a patient on the first floor, when she turned and caught sight of her reflection in the bathroom mirror... and found that it wasn't her own. The young woman fled in terror, never to return. Another unlucky care assistant had taken a nap on her break, in the middle of the night, on a sofa in the communal living room, which was empty and dark at the time. On the floor above, a suspected intruder was running along the corridors and banging the doors loudly. While the rest of the staff went up to investigate, the woman awoke to find herself pinned down as though by the arms of a strong man, and surrounded by a foul smell. It was only when the rest of the staff returned downstairs that she was released, and ran out of the room in terror. Needless to say, there had in fact been no intruder upstairs.

Mr Woods attended many patients in the middle of the night who would point at the corner of their rooms in terror, as though they had seen something which he could not. He noted that this always happened in the oldest wing of the building, and always in the same few rooms, one of which was rumoured to have been the old nursery in the days that the house was a family home. It comes as no surprise that certain patients reported hearing the voices of children, and several claimed to have seen 'strangely dressed' children playing on the lawns outside... although whenever a member of staff looked, there was never anybody there.

An enormous spiral staircase, which gives access to every landing, was reputedly another haunted spot. Many members of staff have felt a cold breeze rush past them in the opposite direction to which they are walking, as though somebody had passed them on the stairs. Mr Woods also noted that one particular door, accessible only from these stairs, had been roughly bricked up, although the door itself had not been removed, and nobody knew the reason why.

Ian Woods' own experiences at this nursing home have been equally chilling. He has felt the hand of 'a small child' ruffle his hair from behind as he sat writing reports in the office in the small hours of one morning, and notes feeling as though he were being watched in the same room. On another occasion, Mr Woods remembers hearing heavy breathing similar to the 'death rattle' - the sound made when a dying person draws his or her final breaths - coming from an empty bathroom, and then again later in the 'sluice room', a room used for washing bed-pans. Uncannily, when he reported his experience to a colleague, she informed him that the last patient to die in the room he had first heard the sound was a lady he had previously known well, and had enquired about shortly before. Was this lady relaying the message of her death to an old friend who had enquired about her after she died? Her breathing had in fact been laboured just before she passed away, similar to the sound Mr Woods described hearing.

Several residents of the same nursing home have also reported seeing a nurse they did not recognise in the middle of the night. Her description met that of a nurse who had died shortly before. And the kitchen area, which is open at all times of the day and night for staff to make drinks, has on several occasions been filled with a strange bluish haze, often associated with spirit activity.

Communications after Death

When Ron Webster was a child, he and his grandfather would stand at the top of the stairs in his mother's house, watching through a small window the World War II bombers fly over the city of Chesterfield. Ron was close to his grandfather, who had fought in the Great War, and they spent many hours together observing the city from their lookout position.

Ron was sixteen when his grandfather died, and shortly afterwards, he came home from the local firm where he was now apprenticed, and walked into the hall to see his grandfather at the top of the stairs, looking out of their favourite window. It was 5.30 pm and still daylight. Ron felt no fear as he approached the solid-looking form of the old man... and started a conversation with him! The pair stood at the top of the stairs for a minute or so exchanging pleasantries, before Ron ran down to find his mother and tell her who he had seen. Naturally she thought that her son was dreaming. When the pair approached the stairs, the old man was nowhere to be seen, but to this day Ron Webster remains convinced that he held a conversation with a dead man.

When Ron was first married, he and his wife Joan lived with her family in an old house on Beetwell Street, Chesterfield. One night they lay in bed asleep when Ron was awoken by a strange chill; he looked over to the side of the bed where a figure was beginning to materialise. It was the form of a young man in a black uniform, wearing riding breeches and wide-cuffed gloves, with rows of silver buttons on his chest. The apparition wore a strange black skull-cap with goggles pulled back over it, and beckoned to Ron before disappearing. The following night, Ron was awoken by a pair of hands closing firmly around his legs, which began to drag him out of bed... and he woke suddenly to see the same apparition, standing at the foot of the bed! When on the third night the figure appeared again, and this time gave Ron a horrible scowl before disappearing, he felt that it was time to tell his wife Joan of his strange experiences.

From his description of the man in the bedroom, Joan's family were able to show him a photograph of her cousin Jack, a young dispatch rider who had been killed in the War. His uniform was just as Ron had vividly described it, and his face was identical to that in the photograph. The black 'skull cap' was a peaked cap turned backwards, and the goggles and gloves were all standard war-time issue. When Joan explained that her cousin had promised to look after her, Ron began to feel that the spectre was trying to somehow scare him away. Joan also recalled seeing, as she lay in bed one night, the spirit of her cousin, wearing identical uniform to that described by her husband. On this occasion, the apparition vanished when she called out to her mother in fear. Fortunately, the apparition of Jack was never seen again, and shortly after Ron's last sighting, the couple moved into a house of their own.

Ron Webster almost died several years ago, when he contracted a double dose of pneumonia. His full recovery took several months, and it was only when his health was returning that he realised he had been close to death for a while. Ron was lying in bed one day, almost fully recovered, when he began to have a vision. The bedroom in front of him began to change into a green field, which stretched away into the distance with a stream and a bridge in the foreground. A cloaked figure came across the bridge towards Ron, and pulled its hood down to reveal the face of his mother, telling him that it was not 'his time to go' yet - and then turned into a bare skull. Ron clearly saw the Grim Reaper's scythe in the figure's hands. It eventually retreated, and the vision ended.

More recently, the Websters visited an historic Cider House in the West Country, which had once been on a main 19th century stagecoach route. The couple often holidayed in this hotel, and had a favourite room to which they returned year after year. However, on this particular occasion, the landlord gave his apologies for the fact that they would have to be relocated in the four-poster room.

Ron and Joan retired to bed at around 11.30 pm, but Ron was woken a couple of hours later feeling a familiar cold chill... and watched the newspaper he had left on the floor only hours before rise several feet into the air before dropping to the ground again. Before his eyes there appeared a tall bearded gentleman wearing a large black hat and tailcoat, with white ruffled cuffs and a flamboyant cravat, who was visible only from the waist up. Ron watched as the figure made its way towards the bed; the figure disturbed Ron's sleeping wife (who turned over restlessly) before it smiled and vanished.

On recounting his tale to the landlord the following morning, Ron found that he was not the only person to have seen the spectre. Several years previously, a barmaid was cutting sandwiches for the beer delivery crew and had counted four people heading into the cellar. When only three reappeared for lunch, she asked where the gentleman in the strange hat had gone to...

The phantom has also been seen leaning against the mantelpiece in the main room of the hotel, watching the customers. Most puzzling of all, nobody has ever seen his legs! He only materialised from the waist up, and is believed to have been a former landlord of the Cider House, who died in an horiffic accident in the 19th century. In days of old when the building was a stagecoaching inn, staff would tend to the coach horses of passing travellers, and trim the coach lamp-wicks and refill the lamps with oil. On one such evening, the former landlord, always resplendent in a large hat and tailcoat and flamboyant cravat, had accidentally poured oil over himself and caught fire, dying in the ensuing blaze. However, rather than being considered a bad omen, the spectre, nicknamed Henry, is thought to bring good luck.

The Sheffield 'Scream'

Sheffield's alias is 'Steel City', and not without reason, for it has been the capital of the British iron and steel industry for over two centuries. The city was famed for its tableware as early as the reign of Henry VIII, and

Sheffield stainless steel cutlery is today exported for use world-wide. Steelworking is still a dangerous trade, as the following story, recounted by the local historian Ernest Baker (who heard it from a Sheffield foundry worker several years ago) reveals.

A gantry crane driver was operating his machine in the rafters of a large foundry, whilst having a disagreement with his controller on the ground below. The driver angrily left his control box, but tragically slipped and fell into a crucible of molten steel below him. Nobody could help him as he plunged to his death, and he was completely cremated in an instant. The ensuing inquest recorded a verdict of accidental death, and the ingot made of the crucible of steel was marked in chalk 'NOT TO BE USED'.

Several years later, the incident remained a distant memory among the older staff, and as the chalk notice wore away, new employees knew nothing of its story. Through oversight, the ingot was eventually sent away to be made into a flywheel for a large power station. The engineers at this station assembled a steam engine using the Sheffield flywheel, but as soon as it was started up a terrifying inhuman scream was heard to come from within. Engineers carried out many tests and checks, even changing the new and expensive bearings, but without avail. Management eventually questioned staff at the foundry where the flywheel had been made, and somebody recalled the 'crane-driver ingot'. It was decided to remove the flywheel in favour of a new one, although it was never scrapped: it was buried with due decorum.

The Derelict House

It has often been suggested that supernatural experiences are more likely had by those people who are sensitive in nature. Although nobody has ever been able to prove whether this is likely to be the case, the following story, told by a Doncaster man several years after it happened, goes some way towards suggesting that this may be true.

Many years ago, when the gentleman who had this experience was just a schoolboy, he and two friends of the same age were out looking for adventure one night, when they decided to enter a dilapidated building in the Doncaster area. This building looked as though it must once have been very fine, although it was boarded up and crumbling, and none of the boys had any idea who owned it. Although the three companions knew that they should not enter, they found their way through a small opening in the darkness and climbed into what must once have been a living room. They had only been there a short while when a 'swishing' noise filled the room, getting gradually louder and louder. The man who recounted this tale told how he looked towards his companions in horror as he became aware of a blue hazy light beginning to fill the room. And as they glanced towards an old stairwell through an open door, the bottom of a lady's glowing skirt came into view, 'swishing' as it fell over the steps.

The three terrified boys scrambled out through the small exit as fast as they could, and it was only when at a safe distance that they stopped to compare stories of what they had just seen. Although two of them had heard the same noises and experienced a chilling sensation as the blue light engulfed the room, and seen the phantom lady's skirts, the third boy had seen and heard nothing... he had merely witnessed the expressions on his companions' faces, and assumed that the police had arrived to apprehend them all!

Herald of Death

During the time that Amy Ward nursed in geriatric wards in hospitals throughout South Yorkshire, a common belief she encountered from many of the older nurses was that, when a patient was about to die, an envoy from the spirit world would come to 'fetch' them. On one occasion, Mrs Ward was sharing a shift with one such older nurse whom she described as very sharp of mind, and not given to exaggeration. A certain patient had been restless all night, and as soon as she was tucked up would get out of bed and wander around the ward. The nurses sat in the corridor, where they had clear vision of the two rooms they were to watch over, through the glass panelling at either side of where they were stationed. Throughout the night they got up countless times to put the restless patient back to bed, until the older nurse exclaimed to Mrs Ward: 'She's up again! And she's standing over Beatrice's bed this time!' With that, she made her way into the room on the left, although Mrs Ward had followed her line of sight and had seen nothing. Her colleague returned with a puzzled expression on her face; the restless woman appeared to be asleep at last, and there had been nobody awake in the ward.

At 3.00 am that morning, the elderly patient, Beatrice, died. Mrs Ward was convinced that her colleague had seen the fabled spirit envoy said to visit the dying; she also noted that she herself saw nothing, despite what the older nurse described.

Whilst working in the same hospital, Mrs Ward on one occasion saw an elderly female patient wearing a hospital nightdress walk towards her as she sat having a cup of tea. She could not tell which patient it was as her head was bowed, so, concerned that somebody was wandering the wards late at night, she went to put the lady to bed... but found the wards quiet and everybody tucked up, soundly asleep.

The Crying Boy Phenomenon

In the mid-1980's, a strange story came to light in the South Yorkshire region concerning a painting known as the 'Crying Boy'. Rotherham fireman Peter Hall noticed that, in a spate of house fires in the area, a common factor seemed to be that there was a copy of the Crying Boy hanging on the wall, and in each case this had remained untouched in the ensuing blaze.

At least six versions of this popular print were in existence, each depicting a young boy who has been captured by the artist in floods of tears. In several cases, whole houses were destroyed by fire and yet the picture remained undamaged.

The Sun newspaper was quick to catch on to this mystery, and invited its readers to write in with their similar experiences. In the resulting publicity, they were contacted by a householder in Herringthorpe who lost his entire home in a blaze; his Crying Boy painting remained unmarked despite pictures which were hanging on either side of it being destroyed. A Nottinghamshire man vowed to destroy his copy when a fire at his home put his wife and two children in hospital.

Fireman Peter Hall's brother Ron refused to take the warning seriously, and left his version of the Crying Boy hanging on the wall of his Swallownest home. Soon afterwards a fire broke out, damaging the kitchen and living room, although the picture remained untouched on the living room wall. Ron Hall put his foot through the picture in fury, and his wife would never allow it to be replaced.

These strange phenomena were not limited to the North Midlands alone. The original question from *The Sun* prompted replies from all over the country from people who had had similar experiences. An Oxfordshire woman was taken to hospital suffering from severe burns, while her Crying Boy remained almost untouched in her charred home. A Pizza Hall in Great Yarmouth was completely gutted by a mysterious fire, and again the Crying Boy on the wall was undamaged.

Rotherham fireman Alan Wilkinson was familiar with the Crying Boy fires, having attended enough of them to have noted for himself the lack of damage to the paintings in otherwise gutted houses. When interviewed by Georgina Boyes for an article in *The Questing Beast*, he told her that he had at one point taken a Crying Boy print into his own fire station. For a while, Mr Wilkinson kept this in his locker, before deciding to put it up in the Station office. On the day he did so, a fire broke out in the station kitchen, burning the entire watch's dinners and needing immediate attention to extinguish it. The fire had been quite serious, and from then onwards even the most unsuperstitious of the firemen made their own excuses as to why they would not possess copies of the Crying Boy.

After the initial outburst of publicity concerning the strange fires believed to be linked to the picture, many people attempted to destroy their versions of the print. A resident of North Anston, a village in the Rotherham area, took her version of the Crying Boy out into the garden and added it to a bonfire of garden rubbish in an attempt to get rid of it. The fire she lit continually extinguished itself, and it too several attempts to destroy the portrait. She was not the only person to have this problem. Janet Wyatt of Wroxall tried to burn her two versions of the painting, which both refused to catch fire. She was forced to dispose of them elsewhere.

Stories of the source of the painting quickly began to emerge when *The Sun* began to enlist the help of experts to explain away the spate of fires. Roy Vickery, Secretary to the British Folklore Society, felt that the original artist 'may have mistreated the child model in some way'. In his own words: 'All these fires could be the child's curse, his way of getting revenge.'

Although nothing further came to light to confirm the speculations, a frenzy of Crying Boy-related fires swept the country before gradually dying down towards the end of the 1980's. It is doubtful whether many Yorkshire residents of today have hung on to their paintings; the widespread publicity was enough to prompt most people to get rid of them quickly.

Refuge House

Moorgate Road is one of Rotherham town centre's oldest roads, and contains a number of fine old buildings which were converted into business properties in the second half of this century. Refuge House is one such building, and staff who work here have noted many strange happenings over a period of several years.

In the early 1990's, salesman Paul Smith was with a colleague in a main office at around 1.00 am in the morning, preparing to finish work after a long shift. Before their eyes a stack of papers rose into the air and began to whirl around as though being blown by a freak draught, in a circular motion. They continued to circle for around fifteen seconds before eventually fluttering to the floor. On another occasion, two employees were preparing to lock up, having ensured that everybody else had left the building, when they were stopped by a pitiful female voice shouting to them from upstairs: 'Don't leave me! Don't lock me in!' The upper floor of Refuge House was once used as servants' quarters when it was still a residential building, and staff have frequently heard footsteps crossing the floor, and doors opening and closing when nobody is actually present on that floor.

Visitation after Death

One February in the early 1990's, Janice Davies, who lives in Laughton-en-le-Morthen, a village in the Rotherham area, had a minor car crash which left her uninjured but shaken. A widow who lives on her own, she was most upset by the incident, but described a strange occurrence which happened shortly afterwards and served to reassure her. In her living room is a large comfortable chair placed next to the gas fire, close to the kitchen door. Janice was walking from the kitchen into the living room when she caught sight of a woman wearing a long skirt, sitting in the chair. Although her face was not visible, as she had her head bowed and appeared to be brushing and neatening her skirt, Janice could see that her hair was grey. As she was most definitely in the house on her own at the time, Janice watched, intrigued but without feeling fear. The vision of the woman disappeared slowly from the feet upwards in front of her eyes, leaving the chair empty. Janice remains convinced that she saw a vision of her mother, who had somehow come to reassure her at a point in her life at which she felt particularly low.

The Nether Edge Haunting

Occasionally, strange events occur which do not seem to fit into any of the usual categories of ghost, poltergeist or 'unexplained' phenomena. It is at this point that a particular story comes to mind, involving a family who until quite recently lived in the Nether Edge area of Sheffield. Paranormal researchers investigated the case for a number of weeks, and found it to be convincing and inexplicable.

Nether Edge housewife June Roberts often had unusual experiences. She had seen UFO's, had an out-of-body experience, and wherever she lived 'teleportation' phenomena seemed to occur. Objects would appear and disappear regularly, so often that Mrs Roberts became accustomed to it. Then, when she was expecting her second child, her house became the focus for a different kind of activity which was to continue for several years.

A strange smoke-like object often appeared in the Roberts' bedroom, always whenever Mrs Roberts was present. She would often reach for her glasses as she lay in bed, having noticed something at her feet which she could not quite focus on, only to be confronted by a moving shapeless haze which she described as containing many flashing, colourless lights comparable to 'the lights one sees when you close your eyes or go dizzy'. Mrs Roberts suffered illness during her pregnancy, and whenever the 'thing' appeared, she noted '...it has always had a calming effect on me, giving me a feeling of peace, I suppose'. On getting out of bed at night, the 'thing' would follow her around the room, and out into the hall. At one point she even walked 'through' the object, and described the feeling as unusually cool and 'light of touch'.

Mrs Roberts did not talk to her husband about her strange experiences, deciding that it would be unwise to worry him. Even after the birth of their young son, when her health returned to normal, she continued to see the misty form with its flashing lights. When she eventually plucked up enough courage to mention it to her husband, he denied having any knowledge of the strange sight, although it later emerged that he in fact had seen a comparable 'moving shadow' himself. One night when her young son was ill and Mrs Roberts had taken him into her own bed, he suddenly said: 'That thing's here again'. Mrs Roberts cautiously asked what he meant, to which the young boy replied: 'Those flashing lights'. It became clear from then onwards that it was not a simple case of imagination, and the sightings were not limited to June Roberts alone.

Neither were paranormal experiences in the house restricted to the family involved. A family friend, Mary, was being shown around the flat when the tour reached the Roberts' bedroom and she suddenly stopped and moved away, refusing to enter the bedroom because there was 'something nasty in there'. A babysitter named Hazel was left on her own one evening when she found the room growing uncomfortably cold; although she saw nothing, she experienced goose-pimples for no reason, and sensed an unusual coolness in the Roberts' bedroom.

The paranormal researchers who were called in to observe the strange case at Nether Edge looked for many varying explanations as to what was causing the appearance of the 'apparition': chemical leakages which could cause hallucination, electrical phenomena, and so on... but nothing came to light. Interestingly, shortly after their attention was drawn to the case, the appearance of the 'thing' dwindled and eventually disappeared altogether. The researchers did note, however, that on their first visit to the Roberts' house, they too were able to detect an atmosphere of unusual coldness in the main bedroom. On their second visit the room was much warmer; Mrs Roberts herself noted that this was the first time that the bedroom had been properly warm since they had moved into the house.

No formal conclusions were ever drawn on the case, and shortly after the researchers completed their study, the Roberts moved further south and lost all contact. Nobody was able to offer any suitable explanation for the mysterious hazy presence which had shared the house in Nether Edge for so many years.

The King Rat

Animal phenomena have been noted in folklore for several centuries, in the form of phantom animals and animal spirits which portend death and disaster, or act protectively, like the mysterious Padfoot. More unusual still are stories which concern the 'King Rat', a nest of living rats tied together in a circle by their tails acting as a live 'throne' for an impossibly large rat which sits among them. This phenomenon has been discovered in underground workings such as sewers and mines several times in the last century, much to the amazement of the surprised onlookers. No explanation has been offered, save that the animal kingdom perhaps displays its own hierarchy in such an unusual way. However, the sighting of large groups of animals being led by a prominent leader is not restricted to the sewers!

When the old Sheffield fish market was being pulled down, a taxi driver in Barkers Pool was amazed to witness literally hundreds of rats making their way down High Street in an enormous stream, headed by a huge 'king rat' whom they all trailed along behind. The number of rats was so vast that the driver stared in fascination for a good while until they had disappeared, and several other witnesses came forward the following day to testify to having seen the same unusual sight.

Message After Death

Rotherham nurse Amy Ward nursed her brother Walter through cancer many years ago, and was the only person present at his death bed. Walter had been a great fan of classical music during his lifetime, particularly opera, which he adored. Several moments after she had watched her brother die, Mrs Ward walked downstairs with the words *Panis Angelicus* running through her mind, and although she was aware that it must be the title of a religious operatic work, at the time she had no knowledge of it; she had neither heard the title nor the music itself. Convinced that her brother was trying to give her some kind of message in the moments after his death, Mrs Ward immediately told the rest of her family that Walter wanted a piece of music called *Panis Angelicus* playing at his funeral. Written by Caesar Franck, and sung and recorded by Pavarotti, Walter's 'request' was granted... and to this day his sister believes it to have been a wish from beyond death.

The Eccentric

It is not hard to imagine how certain ghostly tales can become embroidered over the years, being passed down through generations, the original characters long forgotten. The following story, recounted by Rotherham resident Mr Edward Law (who heard it in the North Nottinghamshire town of Clowne many years ago) is one such example, although it possibly dates from the early 1950's - which, as folk tales go, makes it relatively modern!

'During the early 1950's, a newspaper boy on his weekday round in Clowne was regularly greeted at the door of a particular house by its solitary occupant, an amiable man who always had a pleasant greeting and who, despite being a simpleton, managed to look after himself. The old man never bothered a soul, spending most of his days walking the lanes and footpaths around Clowne. He loved to talk to people but because he was considered by most folk to be only 'nine pence to the shilling' they tended to shun conversation with him, limiting their words to a bare minimum as they passed. Over the years, with no-one to have a good natter with, he turned to talking to himself, having full-blown arguments with himself on whatever subject took his fancy.

Because of this, his simplicity, and the fact he had a strong, loud voice, he was shunned even more. Only the newspaper boy found the time to indulge his passion for talking and limited though he was for time in a morning, he made the old chap's house his last call, and over a hot cup of strong tea, mainly listened to the outpourings of a lonely man.

'For almost two years the pair exchanged daily greetings and Saturday chats that rarely lasted above half an hour; then the newspaper boy left school and joined the Navy, seeking his fortune sailing the world. Before he left, he made one last visit to the old man to tell him of his plans, and promised to call and see him when home on leave.

'It was eighteen months before the young man, resplendent in his naval uniform, returned to Clowne, alighting at the bus station to stagger beneath the weight of his kitbag as he walked the final part of his journey home. By strange coincidence, as he turned into the street where his parents lived, the first person he bumped into was the old man.

'Not wishing to have to stand and chat after a long journey carrying heavy luggage, but afraid of upsetting the elderly simpleton, the young man gave him a smile, a cheery hello, and asked briefly how he had been keeping. As if sensing the young man's need to hurry, and not wanting to delay him, the elderly eccentric smiled back and with a wave of his hand called out simply, "Bless you ma duck, bless you."

'Two days later the young man was walking through Clowne when he happened to pass the old man's house and, deciding that he had time, chose to fulfil his promise and pay him a visit. A neighbour heard the young man's determined knocking and opened his door, explaining that no amount of banging would induce a reply: the old man had died several months previously.'

The Figure in Black

Ann Jones works as a care assistant with the elderly, which involves tending to residential patients on a shift basis. She often works late into the night, and on one such occasion in 1995, had almost reached the end of her shift and was preparing for the staff changeover. A patient named Gladys had given Ann's shift cause for concern, and when the night staff arrived, she and her Charge Nurse filled them in on the details. Gladys had been restless but was now asleep in a chair; she had asked Ann to 'take her' earlier on, and when Ann asked where, she had pointed to the main door. Puzzled, Ann had settled her down again until she fell asleep.

The doors and windows had been open all day due to the summer heat, although they had later been locked and secured as darkness fell. The Charge Nurse suddenly shouted: 'Who's that who's just walked through the lounge? The outside door must be open!'

Although nobody else present had seen anything, the Charge Nurse insisted that a very tall man, dressed in black, had run into the lounge and towards the exit. Concerned for Gladys, who had been asleep in a chair, they checked the room but found nobody there, and saw the old lady still peacefully asleep. Ann and her colleagues checked the main door and found it locked. The Charge Nurse was by now very concerned, and assured the others that there was no way she had imagined the tall gentleman, having definitely seen him leave through the main exit. Although this particular nurse was new to the residential home, she was aware that other staff had often heard and felt a presence there. She is now convinced of the truth of their tales.

Was the man in black in some way associated with the elderly patient Gladys? Ann's own experience of a black figure some years earlier led her to believe that he was, although figures in black do not always seem to act as 'heralds of death' as has often been suggested, and as the following story shows.

Ann was bathing an elderly blind lady one evening with a colleague, the three of them chatting away cheerfully, when she felt something touch her shoulder. She turned and froze, for against the white tiles of the bathroom wall behind her, she saw a tall faceless figure all in black, whom she somehow felt to be male. Ann recalls hearing her colleague repeating her name, and became aware that the elderly blind lady had suddenly become silent and still, as though she too sensed something. She remained frozen for what seemed to her like an eternity, until she turned back to her colleague with such an expression on her face that her co-worker: 'Good God, what have you seen? Your face is stony grey!' Ann remained speechless as they dressed the resident and took her to her room, waiting until later to tell her colleague what had happened. This lady had seen nothing, but had locked the bathroom door on their entry rendering it impossible for anybody else to have got into the room.

Strangely, when Ann recovered from the initial shock of her experience, she recalls having felt 'so calm, peaceful and light... I got a feeling he was a kind presence. He hadn't come to call on my old lady; she remained with us, for a while anyway.'

The Haunted Wood

A Doncaster metal-detecting enthusiast with a particular fondness for searching ancient woodland recounted the following tale, which took place in the early 1980's. While on a walk in the countryside, Darren Dray noticed an old stretch of woodland which immediately aroused his interest. Although he had never searched this area before, on previous visits to similar sites he had unearthed old coins, artefacts and ammunition. He therefore decided to trace the owner of the land, and requested permission to visit with his metal-detector. Although the farmer appeared uneasy about the request, he gave his consent.

A few days later, with his detector set up and tuned in, Mr Dray set off into the wood. He had travelled about ten yards into the foliage when he was suddenly overcome by a feeling of intense cold. Removing his earphones, he noticed that the area was unusually quiet. He later noted that 'there was no sound of birds or the rustle of animal life, such as rabbits or squirrels - just an uncanny stillness.' He convinced himself that it must be his imagination, put on the earphones again, and continued further into the wood. Another three yards on, and in addition to the feeling of coldness, Mr Dray's scalp began to tingle and he was overcome by an irrational feeling of terror. He turned off his metal-detector and retreated hastily.

Once at home, Mr Dray rationalised his thoughts and became convinced that he had most likely frightened himself. He therefore decided to return to the wood, although this time to a different location. A few days later he managed to get slightly further than on his previous visit. However, the familiar cold feeling soon overtook him, his scalp once again began to tingle, and as he continued to move forwards through the undergrowth, the feeling of fear mounted within him. In his own words, 'I could not control or describe it, only that I wanted to run like hell out of the wood, to get away from the fear. Once again I left the wood in a sorry state.'

Mr Dray related his story to a friend who was also a keen metal-detecting hobbyist. This friend was totally unconvinced by the tale which was related, and suggested that they both return to the wood together to prove that the experience had been imaginary. Several days later, the pair visited the site and commenced their search in good spirits, chatting as they walked through the trees.

After a few yards, Mr Dray began to feel uneasy, and glanced towards his friend. This man too looked a little jumpy, although he showed no sign of wanting to stop. They continued, until a little further on 'it was there again, the coldness, the fear, the hair tingling... my friend said that he felt the same as I. We both agreed there must be an answer, so we went further into the wood, and managed to get another ten yards, but by then the fear was so great that I was on the verge of panic. Suddenly my friend turned and ran - he could stand it no longer. I was not far behind.'

In medieval times, Devils were apparently not above abducting innocent maidens

The two men headed out of the wood as fast as they could, and afterwards recounted how they had stood 'staring at each other as white as ghosts, sweating with fear'. They were so terrified by the feelings they had encountered that it was a good while before they could even utter a word. The friend who had originally been sceptical admitted that he had never felt fear like that before, so much so that he had thought he was going mad.

With their curiosity aroused, but by now far too frightened to ever enter the wood again, Mr Dray decided to pay a visit to the farmer who owned the land and had initially given him permission to search the woods, to enquire about the site. When he did so, and told the farmer what had happened on three separate visits there, he was met with a knowing look. The farmer explained that he had initially been uneasy about granting permission to search the wood for this very reason; over the years both his father and grandfather had tried to clear the trees to extend their growing land, but to no avail. Nobody would return to the area after their first visit. The land has remained unchanged here for centuries, although nothing is known about the site, and it remains untouched to this day.

An old engraving of Wharncliffe Crags, now cut through by the Stocksbridge Bypass

*The alehouse has been the focus of English social life since medieval times:
small wonder then, that some 'regulars' refuse to let a little thing like death
stop them popping into their 'local'.*

Haunted Pubs

The following selection of haunted public houses only scratches the surface of a wealth of other such places in and around South Yorkshire. Traditionally, most pubs are old buildings with a great deal of history, many of which have been converted for their purpose at some point, so perhaps it comes as no surprise to find that they often have occupants from the past!

The White Swan

'Come tomorrow and you shall have good ale for nothing. Do not forget - 1686' reads an inscription on the outside wall of one of the oldest public houses in Maltby. Originally The Swan, in 1880 this old stone building took its current name, and has expanded to take over neighbouring premises in recent years. The main bar area was once the local coaching inn, and the intricate maze of rooms in the cellar show signs of having once been a cavernous kitchen, complete with an ancient fireplace and curved-ceiling storage rooms.

Local legend has it that the cellar of the White Swan hides the entrance to a tunnel which once ran to the nearby church of St Bartholomews. Legends of such subterranean passages are common in many old buildings, notably public houses, old churches, castles and abbeys. Many possibly acted as escape routes for the clergy and nobility in times of religious and political persecution.

The current landlord, Ray Robinson, and his three predecessors have all experienced strange goings-on inside the building, with additional reports from customers, bar staff and relief tenants alike. Several of the current staff refuse to visit the cellar alone to change barrels, reporting strange noises, the feeling of being watched, phantom footsteps, and even a curious male voice which asks, 'What are you doing?' On turning to answer him, members of staff have found nobody there. Mr Robinson's office is based in the cellar (which his wife refuses to enter when alone) and he too, in the small hours of the morning, has heard the creeping approach of a person unknown across the stone floor.

On one occasion, a barmaid was horrified to see a bottle whizzing past her head from the shelf behind the bar, which landed in a stack of clean glasses, smashing them. The bottle had been part of a display (now removed for safety!) and could not have fallen so violently, or have been pushed, as it was against the wall. On another occasion, a figure in old-fashioned clothing was seen by one of the current staff, crossing the room and disappearing through an adjoining wall.

This is similar to a tale told by an earlier landlord, in which he had emptied the bar of all except a handful of regulars one Sunday afternoon, when a woman walked across the room in front of them and out through the side door. None of the regulars took much notice, until the landlord returned to tell them that the pub was finally empty, and one man commented that he had just seen the last woman leave. The mystery woman had not passed the landlord on her way out, as she should have done on her way from the other bar, and the door she left through had been locked by the landlord much earlier!

Ray Robinson admitted to having been sceptical when he first moved into the White Swan in 1992; two of his predecessors had told him spooky tales of happenings in the pub, but he preferred to disbelieve them and consider that everything had a rational explanation. His views were soon to change, however. The office had only one key, which Mr Robinson had been warned by a previous landlord not to lose as there was no duplicate. This was kept on a large key-chain in Mr Robinson's pocket. One evening he had unlocked the office to take some till change from the safe. He went to the bar to replenish the till, then realised that he needed something from the office. Mr Robinson returned... to find the door locked. Assuming that he must have relocked it earlier, he searched for the key but could not find it. Both Mr Robinson and his wife combed all possible areas of the pub and their living quarters for the next half-an-hour in an attempt to find the keys, but they were nowhere to be seen. Eventually, the couple resorted to hunting around in some of the old crockery left in one of the upstairs rooms where they knew that several old keys had been left, hoping that one of these would fit. Amazingly one did - and as Mr Robinson entered the office he saw his own bunch of keys lying on top of the safe! As the office door was not a self-locking door, the couple realised that it was impossible for the door to have been re-locked when the keys were inside all the time.

One of the upstairs bedrooms, which the family cat has always refused to enter, has an unusually chilly atmosphere. When the Robinsons first moved in, they took this room as their bedroom. Two weeks later, they decided that there was something strange about the place, and moved into an adjoining room. Previous landlords had also commented on this, although Mr Robinson originally chose to disbelieve them. Talking to an old regular customer in the bar one evening, he discovered rumours that the ghost of a child, said to have died in this room many years ago, is allegedly in residence. On numerous occasions, the Robinsons have been woken in the night by the sound of a crying child which has proved impossible to locate. At first the couple suspected that their cat was responsible for the sounds. Then, a relief manager who knew nothing of the story took over the White Swan for a fortnight... and on the Robinsons' return, asked if they had ever been troubled by the inexplicable noises of a crying child.

A mysterious male voice, which was heard by Mrs Robinson, called out to her one afternoon as she lay in the bath. At first she assumed that it was her husband calling from downstairs. When he did not appear, she was puzzled - even more so when she found out that he had been in the cellar office the whole time! Strange sights and sounds continue at the White Swan to this day, making it an ideal starting point for a tour of South Yorkshire's haunted pubs.

The Old Crown

The Old Crown at Great Houghton, near Barnsley, seems an unlikely place to find a spectre, having only been built in the 1960's. However, in 1994, landlady Edna Seaton had gone downstairs to open up at 7pm when she was shocked to see a shadowy figure in the shape of a tall man pass by the bar. Edna described the spectre as 'too light in substance' to be a real person - and in any case the outside doors were still locked, and there was no way anybody could have entered (or left) the bar.

Edna Seaton is not the only one to have had such an experience; a visitor to the pub several years ago was in the cellar when he allegedly felt an invisible presence and left in a hurry. Despite her continued scepticism, Edna is also aware that former bar staff have in fact had similar encounters, and she herself now refuses to open up on dark nights without full lighting on.

The Red Rum

A similar story attaches to the Red Rum public house in Barnsley, which is believed to be haunted by the spetre of a woman thought to have died there in the last century. Doors have helpfully opened themselves for people to walk through, and cleaners and customers alike have spotted a lady in long skirts, who appears and disappears suddenly. In 1990, regular customer Wayne Clarke was about to leave the Red Rum one night, after last orders, when he was astonished to see a stranger walk through the bar. Knowing that nobody could have entered the premises, and the doors were locked, he quickly described what he had seen to the landlady ... who confirmed that he had indeed seen the resident ghost! Wayne noticed that the woman was dressed in an old fashioned manner, in long skirts and a cap. There had been several similar sightings of the Red Rum's resident ghost over the years, though her exact identity remains a mystery.

Cromwells Restaurant

A short distance from St Peter's Church in Conisbrough there stands an unusual old building which appears at first glance to be Georgian in origin. Further investigation into its architecture reveals that the old house, now a restaurant called Cromwells, has much earlier roots, and is believed to have been built during the 1600's.

Throughout its history, the building has had many uses - as a farmhouse, a boarding school, a post office, and a community centre. In 1983 it was sold on to become what is today a licensed restaurant, although unfortunately a rather unexpected visitor from the past was handed down along with the deeds of the property, much to the surprise of the current staff!

Before recent alterations changed the interior of the building, the stairwell leading to the upstairs bar was next to a narrow passage. Chef Ian Godfrey recounted how one of the waiters was surprised one afternoon by a figure in a long cloak and a large hat with a feather, rushing past him as he made his way down the stairs. The figure, similar in appearance to a Cavalier, disappeared in an instant, leaving the waiter startled. It is perhaps no coincidence that an unseen hand has on occasion slammed the kitchen doors on unsuspecting staff, causing them to drop handfuls of plates.

Another local legend tells how one of the former occupants of the house in days of old was involved in an affair with a local man. When her husband found out, she is said to have hanged herself from one of the ceiling beams near the stairs. This area is close to the old coffee lounge, where strange atmospheres and icy coldness have been detected.

When renovations were taking place in 1989, an electrician was rewiring in the upper part of the building in semi-darkness. He was so convinced that a man had walked past him and disappeared that he dropped his tools and ran downstairs to confront his colleague, whom he suspected of playing tricks. Assured that this was not the case, the electrician then realised that the figure he saw had been wearing old-fashioned clothes, with sacking gaiters on his legs! The history of the building shows that it was used periodically as a working farmhouse for more than two hundred years. The dress of the apparition would suggest that he was a landworker, and his appearance has been recorded on several occasions since.

The current landlord was preparing to close the premises at the end of a busy evening, when all except two of the guests had left the downstairs restaurant. Without warning, a huge gust of air 'screeched' past their heads and 'banged' into the wall close to the chimney. Although the sound was so loud that the remaining guests left in terror, nothing was physically seen, and no explanation could ever be offered.

The Crofts

The Crofts public house, in Mosborough, opened in the late 1980's. Within days the staff were being bombarded by customers' tales of a phantom horse whose appearance near the car park almost caused them to crash. The animal would materialise suddenly on the tarmac (several unlucky motorists found themselves slamming on their brakes and swerving at the last moment to avoid it) before it disappeared into thin air. Several of the witnesses declared that a pony and trap had appeared in front of them as they entered the car park. Within a short while the staff had so many complaints on their hands that they decided further action was needed, to avoid the possibility of a serious accident. Fortunately, with a little background research, the haunted history of The Crofts was soon discovered, and preventative steps were taken to ensure that the phantom animals were laid to rest...

The Crofts was constructed on the site of a farmhouse which dated back to 1707. Further research showed that the pond, which was situated in the corner of a neighbouring field, acted as a watering hole for local farm horses. After a day working the land, farmhands would drive their carts down to the pond where the wagons could be washed and the horses could take a drink. When the car park of The Crofts was constructed, it was situated right across the old route down to the pond! As soon as the landlord realised that this was the heart of the problem, and that spectral ponies and wagons were still making their evening trip to the local watering hole despite the passage of time, he took steps to dissuade them... by filling the pond in!

The Mill of the Black Monks

This ancient building in Cundy Cross, just outside Barnsley, was originally a watermill. Built in 1150 by the Cluniac Monks from nearby Monk Bretton Priory, it passed into the hands of the Benedictines, and in the 17th century the mill was taken over by the Quakers. The building lay in ruins for many years before extensive renovations returned its former glory, and today it is a beautiful roadside tavern.

Rather than its haunted history putting off the drinkers, psychic experts who have claimed to be in contact with the Mill's several ghosts have encouraged the curious to visit. Conversion work, which began in 1991, saw a number of disturbances - a common factor in haunted houses. Barmaids have described how unseen hands have touched them, and white shapes have floated through the walls. Customers have seen small objects such as ashtrays and glasses move of their own free will, and the figure of a 'solid-looking' ghostly monk standing in the shadows has manifested itself on several occasions.

The phantom monk is not alone in his haunting of the site: the spirits of a church minister and a teenage girl also share his domain! One psychic researcher claimed that he had persuaded the phantom monk to leave the site, but explained that he would be able to 'bring him back' again and communicate at length at some point. Whether you believe in ghosts or not, the atmosphere inside the Mill of the Black Monks is something to be sampled at leisure; many fine old beams and ancient stone walls add to the character of the place, and in summer, the picturesque beer garden is well worth a visit.

The Saxon Hotel

This public house in Kiveton reputedy has a haunted cellar, occupied by a whistling ghost by the name of Jasper. Shortly after its construction in 1960, on an area which is rich in history and was once supposedly the site of a religious establishment, three policemen were called in to spend the night in the cellar after being alerted about strange happenings which had no logical explanation. Despite the policemen hearing nothing on their vigil (much to their relief), several landlords since have reported a mysterious presence which often whistles to them while they are alone in the cellar, and unearthly footsteps which occur when the area is supposedly empty.

The ghost of Jasper is reputed to be that of a monk who once lived in a house now buried beneath the foundations of The Saxon. Whatever his identity, he seems to take pleasure in whistling for attention, although he never reveals himself!

Carbrook Hall

Carbrook Hall, on Attercliffe Common in Sheffield, is proud of its haunted history and is Sheffield's self-styled 'most haunted public house'. Its name stems from the Saxon or Celtic 'brook on the carr', or 'meadow stream'. Visitors to the building, which has 12th century foundations, will be delighted by the Tudor-style panelling in the parlour area and the beautiful plasterwork on the old ceilings. And if you do believe in ghosts, the current landlord is a wealth of information concerning the many strange sightings which have occurred here.

The Parliamentarian John Bright resided at Carbrook in the mid-1600's, being one of Cromwell's most distinguished soldiers during the Civil War. As can be seen from the small stone-framed windows in the parlour, the thickness of the walls is more than two feet... a safety measure in a building which has seen many anti-Royalist meetings, and even welcomed the mighty Cromwell himself. The Hall remained in the Bright family for several generations, eventually being sold in 1819. Later records describe Carbrook as a 'common beer house'!

There are rumours of a secret tunnel which is said to run from Sheffield Castle to Carbrook Hall. Mary Queen of Scots was imprisoned for many years in the Castle, and it is said that whenever it was thought to be under siege, she would be transported underground to the safety of the Hall. If this was ever the case, then it would seem that Carbrook had Royalist sympathies at some point in its history.

Members of the Society for Psychical Research have visited Carbrook Hall on several occasions, hoping to witness some of the supernatural activity for themselves. A former landlady reported seeing the spectre of a Roundhead in a black cap and white collar accompanying the researchers on one of their tours. The current landlord was surprised one evening by the stocky figure of a man wearing heavily draped clothing, who appeared at the top of the stairs as he was climbing them. As the landlord moved aside for the figure to pass, he felt it brush his arm and his hair stood on end. The apparition reached the bottom of the stairs and vanished.

The historic Black Oak Room is to be found upstairs, although this is not open to the public. It was closed many years ago when paranormal experiences frightened previous tenants, although the current landlord now uses it as a bedroom! In the early 1990's, the landlord remembers being woken at 2.30 am by the sounds of children playing outside. On recounting this experience to a local, the old gentleman described how, in the 1920's, the area of land outside Carbrook Hall had been a recreation ground on which the local children used to play. Had he heard a ghostly 'tape-recording' of the past?

The Black Oak Room was once a function room, and was used by local lads for band practices. This abruptly came to a halt one evening when the spectre of a gentleman wearing Civil War uniform approached them, and just as suddenly, disappeared. One of the young men who had experienced this later described the apparition to the current landlord, who was amazed that the description tallied exactly with the 'stranger on the stairs' who he had experienced more recently.

Several of the bar staff have seen a shadow pass through the bar area from the door and disappear into a corner - while the outside door remains unopened and nobody else is in the area. The outside lighting switches are housed in a cleaners' cupboard which is kept locked, although the landlord has turned this off and locked the cupboard on many occasions, only to find the lights back on again as he lets the last person out of the pub. Objects have been seen to move themselves in the bathroom: a bottle of shampoo recently moved across the windowsill and jumped into the bath! The ladies' toilets have the habit of locking their occupants in from time to time, and several terrified women have only been able to escape when another person has entered the room. Canine visitors have the habit of barking at one particular corner in the upstairs living room, and appear to watch something which none of the human occupants can see. An elderly lady in 1920's clothing has been spotted sitting in a chair in one of the upstairs rooms, and both the landlord and his wife have been approached by phantom footsteps while lounging on the sunbed. Each time they have assumed that the other one was creeping up to surprise them... before getting up to find the room empty and the door still locked.

One 'sensitive' visitor to Carbrook Hall believes that some of the disturbances were caused by the finding of several cauldrons which were once bricked up in the wall, at the very point in the bar at which bottles were hurled out onto the floor by an unseen hand. More recently, a hooded figure resembling a monk has been spotted passing through the building.

Carbrook Hall would seem to have a valid claim to being the 'most haunted pub in Sheffield', and current staff and visitors alike report unusual happenings on a fortnightly basis.

The Woodseats Hotel

Situated on Chesterfield Road in Woodseats, Sheffield, parts of this building date back several centuries. A catalogue of paranormal phenomena have been recorded here over the years.

One landlord recounted how he had been forced to the floor by unseen hands while working alone in the cellar. A later landlady was pushed up against the bar in the same manner, although there have never been any clear sightings of whatever was responsible. Objects have been thrown around by an invisible force, including a panful of food which was lifted from the cooker and hurled across the dining room! Children's voices have been heard on several occasions emanating from unoccupied parts of the pub, shrieking and giggling.

Not limiting itself to moving objects around, the Woodseats Hotel spook has also been known to turn the gas supply on and off, and creates eerie 'cold spots' and ghostly tapping noises on an upstairs bedroom door. Perhaps this has something to do with a story remembered by some of the regular customers, in which a child was reputedly burned to death many years ago in one of the upstairs bedrooms. In late 1993, the tenants became so concerned about strange happenings in the Hotel that they decided to call in the experts, and have its rooms blessed.

The Blue Bell Inn

The Blue Bell in Harthill was built in 1923, although it occupied the site of a much earlier building, believed to be several centuries old. In the mid-1980's, a piano was kept in the lounge bar where guest pianists entertained each Saturday night. Imagine landlady Sylvia Ward's horror when she had retired to bed one night, only to be woken by the sounds of the piano playing itself in the room below her, despite the pub being empty! The same few notes were being repeated over and over again, and Mrs Ward admitted to being so terrified that she cringed under the bedcovers rather than heading downstairs to investigate. Eventually there was a loud crash as though the piano lid had been slammed down, and the noises ceased. Strangely enough, one of the ladies' toilets had locked itself from the inside on several occasions prior to this happening, forcing landlord Mike Ward to go in armed with a screwdriver to sort out the problem!

The Don Field Tavern

In the early 1980's, David and Cathy Wayland, tenants of the Don Field Tavern on Eldon Road, Eastwood, were plagued by the spirit of an ex-landlady who had allegedly died on the premises many years before. The ghostly woman appeared to Mrs Wayland one evening dressed in white. She was in her sixties, with dark hair and dark skin, and expressed a desire to stay within the building.

Alongside this sighting were other events which could not easily be explained away... the burglar alarm often activated itself and the toilet lights switched themselves on and off without warning, frightening customers. Doors were locked and unlocked without human assistance, and strange noises terrified the Waylands in the dead of night. The upstairs corridor was one place the family dog would never visit alone, as it was supernaturally cold even when the rest of the building felt warm.

Mr Wayland commented: 'At first these strange goings-on didn't bother me, but now it's unnerving. It's eerie. I can never get the place warm even if I leave the gas fires on.'

The Three Tuns

This Sheffield public house was a city centre watering hole as early as the 1700's, and it is thought that an ancient tavern existed on the site even earlier still. Several of the landlords have only been in residence for a very short time, before requesting that they be moved on to another tenancy. Many visitors to the pub have also experienced strange phenomena, which seem to be restricted to an area in the cellar where some wooden steps lead between rooms. A brewery training officer who asked to be shown around began to shiver and sweat on entering the cellar, and after being taken back upstairs made her excuses to leave - only to have four days off work ill to recover. A young painter who was working in the cellar passed out there, blaming it on the 'flu, although strangely he was fine as soon as he left the building. Another contractor who was working in the cellar left in a hurry after saying that 'something' had touched him on the shoulder. He left his tools and sent someone else to finish the job. Several other people have since felt a mysterious, gentle hand being placed on their shoulder.

None of the cats and dogs who have been in residence at the Three Tuns over the years have dared venture near to the wooden steps in the cellar. Indeed, many people (even those who know nothing of the pub's haunted history) express a strange reluctance to venture in this area of the pub. The sobbing of an unseen woman emanates from this very place, her distressed voice being heard between the hours of midnight and early morning, although her identity remains a mystery.

The Loyal Trooper

South Anston's quiet oak-beamed 17th century pub is situated close to its historic Saxon/Norman Church. The Loyal Trooper is adjoined by a row of stone buildings which were once an abattoir. Despite the fact that these were long since converted into houses, from time to time ghostly cattle which still await their slaughter have been known to materialise!

Although the current landlord has not experienced any strange phenomena within the pub himself, members of his staff have seen fresh pints tipped over slowly and purposefully by an unseen hand, and small objects move around on shelves. Several years ago, one horrified customer testified to having seen a pair of ghostly legs making their way through into the bar area!

The Hermit Inn

In the late 1970's, this old stone public house in Higham, Barnsley, created public interest and hit the headlines when it was taken over by former engineer Michael Wall and his wife Christine. Within a couple of weeks of being installed there, the couple became so terrified that they vowed to leave, if the exorcism they had planned did not work.

Events began when a yellow, glowing face appeared one night on a bedroom wall upstairs, which began to expand and distort, and then disappeared. Mr Wall said of the face: 'You can't really make out the features, but it seems to have two dark areas where the eyes should be. The first time I saw it was shortly after we moved into the pub. I'm a heavy sleeper and don't usually wake, but there was a banging noise. I opened my eyes and saw the face on the wall. It was only there for a few seconds but it really frightened me. After seeing it again, we moved our bed into another bedroom. I had just erected a clothes rail in the corner of the room. Banging woke me in the middle of the night again and I saw the face on the wall. Also, the rail had collapsed.'

Mr Wall said nothing to his wife on this occasion for fear of frightening her even more, although soon afterwards the couple resorted to sleeping with the lights on all night. Shortly later the face appeared again, this time grey in colour, against a brightly lit wall... then rose to the ceiling and disappeared. Pub owner Mr J Nolan promised to make exorcism arrangements immediately, although the Lister family, who had run The Hermit for fifty years previously, had never reported any such problems.

A witch feeding her familiars

Witchcraft And Fairy Lore In And Around South Yorkshire

This small but varied selection of tales, some old and some dealing with more recent happenings, show how superstition prevails in the most unlikely places in and around South Yorkshire. The ancient belief in witchcraft lives on in recent discoveries of places of non-Christian worship, and stories involving white witchcraft and clairvoyancy add another dimension to a little understood, and often feared, subject. Likewise, most modern readers would dismiss a belief in fairies as childish. Yet stories concerning mysterious moving lights in Bleaklow, 'fairy fires' around ancient trees, and haunted barrows all have one thing in common: their association with ancient and half-remembered fairy lore...

Fairies - Myth or Reality?

Everybody is acquainted with the popular image of fairies. For children all over Yorkshire, they are the little people who leave money underneath pillows in exchange for a milk-tooth. In times of old, fairies were the tricksters who stole babies, soured milk and played other tricks on country folk. The infamous Cottingley fairies, photographed earlier this century by two young girls, were never conclusively proved fakes, until as an old lady one of the photographers responsible went public to declare how they had been painted on pieces of cardboard! Not surprisingly, there are few rational folk today who would be prepared to take fairy stories seriously.

It has been suggested that the true origin of the fairy legend stems from the pre-history of the population of Britain. Fairies have long since been associated with barrows - ancient burial mounds which are found

country-wide. Yorkshire and Derbyshire at one time had a fine selection of such prehistoric earthworks, although most of these have been destroyed over a period spanning several hundred years. It was generally believed that Long Barrows, whose inhabitants had the elongated skulls of the New Stone Age people, gave rise to legends of tall folk, elves and giants, long after the barrows' original purpose had been forgotten. Round Barrows were constructed by the Pechts or Picts, a small, dark race said to be nocturnal, secretive, and rumoured to dwell underground, making it easy to see why they became associated with 'fairies'. Fairies have long been believed to dance in rings, often on Round barrows, leaving flowers in the shape of a circle wherever they had gathered. Unusually small finds such as stone arrowheads (nicknamed 'elf bolts'), spindle-whorls ('adder stones') and tiny clay tobacco pipes around barrows fuelled speculation as to their origin.

Fairy Barrows

When the Romans settled in Britain, they showed a marked interest in the contents of ancient tombs which had previously existed undisturbed as part of the landscape. The Romans excavated out of curiosity. Later, Norman monks were convinced that the same sites held the relics of long-dead saints. One barrow opened at Ludlow in 1199 contained three skeletons which the clergy took to belong to early Irish saints. These were duly removed to be interred in a local churchyard, where people flocked in droves in the hope of finding miracle cures! Doubtless they would have been disappointed to find that the skeletons were most likely Neolithic. In later medieval England, royal permission was often given for barrows to be opened up by teams of diggers who were searching for treasure.

The 18th century historian William Stukeley conducted his own research into barrow burials, although archaeology in the 1700's left rather more to be desired than its modern counterpart, and he doubtless destroyed much valuable evidence in his searches. The conclusions Stukeley drew were as steeped in superstition and myth as the notions of the Norman monks had been. He categorised barrows into 'druid', 'priest', and 'priestess' burial chambers, perpetuating the several-hundred year old myth that these ancient mounds had a mystical significance. In the light of this, perhaps it comes as no surprise that even today people look upon these sites with a sense of awe.

The 1800's saw a boom in amateur archaeology. Teams of Victorian gentlemen cut away swathes of earth in an attempt to find out what many of the last undisturbed barrows in England contained. Although a number of people had reasonable methods of excavation, sadly, many more merely desecrated the old tombs. Farmers whose land contained barrows demanded that any gold or silver was yielded up to them by the excavation team on its discovery, despite the fact that little treasure of monetary value was ever found.

Hidden treasure was also assumed to be stored in the domain of the fearsome dragon (a very real terror in the Medieval mind), and so several myths grew up together around the barrows of England. They were not only the burial mounds of sacred folk - they contained wealth beyond imagination, were protected by dragons, and housed fairies who appeared at certain times to dance in rings!

The Bradfield Fairy Pipes

The Peak village of Bradfield, on the outskirts of Sheffield, is well-known for its pre-Norman burial mound, which stands just behind Bradfield Church. Legends of fairies inhabiting the mound have survived through the ages. This superstition was common in the 19th century,when Sheffield historian Reverend Gatty found 'upwards of a hundred specimens' of tiny white clay tobacco pipes, when looking for flint tools in a nearby field. These pipes were held in folk belief to have been made by fairies, since their tiny proportions made them unsuitable for human use. They are still occasionally found near old earthworks such as the Bradfield barrow, although historians are unsure of their original purpose.

Shortly after his discovery of the 'fairy pipes', Reverend Gatty wrote to a friend: 'The fairies are supposed to smoke but where they get their tobacco from is a secret. Certainly the pipes are quite small enough for such small folk, and I have some specimens quite absurd in size... my old clerk at Bradfield used to argue the point with a friend over a pint of beer.' Most modern readers would quite understandably dismiss this as 'superstitious nonsense'; after all, even this century's fairy story concerning the Cottingley Fairy Photographs was revealed as a hoax. However, this makes the following tale all the more intriguing...

In the early 1990's, a young couple were enjoying a walk around the deserted Bradfield barrow at twilight when they suddenly became aware of the sensation of 'many pairs of eyes' watching them from the overgrown mound of earth. The noise of the wind disappeared suddenly into silence, and the atmosphere around the old earthwork became most uncomfortable. Despite having no knowledge of the fairy connotations of the barrow at that time, the couple felt frightened enough to leave the area immediately.

S. O. Addy noted, in *Folk Tales and Superstition*, that 'It is not unlikely that the numerous small tobacco pipes to which the name of "fairy pipes" has been given, and which are so often found upon or near old earthworks, were intended as gifts to the fairies, otherwise the local deities or spirits of the dead'. He himself owned one such small pipe made of white clay, which had been found near the burial mound at Bradfield.

The Grey Ladies

On Harthill Moor, in Derbyshire, stand the remains of The Grey Ladies, otherwise known as the Nine Stones Close. Long believed by some to have been connected with Druidic Ritual, the remains of this prehistoric monument also have fairy associations.

The 19th century historian Llewellyn Jewitt wrote: '...around this Druidical circle it is said - and believed by some of the people of the district - that fairies meet on certain occasions... the full moon, I believe, at midnight and dance and hold "high jubilee". So firmly this is believed that I have been told with extreme seriousness of people who, passing at that time of night, have not only seen the dance but heard the "fairy pipes" playing for them to dance to. I have heard it seriously affirmed that there were hundreds of fairies, gentlemen and ladies, some dancing, other sitting on the stones or on the grass around and others playing music...'

The 'Fates' of Coal Aston

There has long been a legend associated with the appearance of three mysterious fairy women known as the 'Three Fates', or the 'Norns'. They were supposed to appear in portent of the death of a member of the family or indeed the person who sighted them. A resident of Coal Aston described them vividly in the 19th century, as 'three tall, thin women standing in a line with three hour-glasses in their hands'. The hour-glasses symbolised the amount of time left on earth to the victim. The gentleman who gave this account firmly believed that the Three Fates appeared on Coal Aston Common to foretell the deaths of local people. Other versions of the belief describe the 'Norns' as young and beautiful, two dressed in white, and the other in green.

Fairy Customs in the North

North Derbyshire colliers of the 19th century would leave a hundred-weight of coal in certain areas of the mine each week for the 'fairies', or mine-spirits. Another Yorkshire custom concerned the picking of wild fruits. People out gathering blackberries would always cast their first pick over their shoulder as a gift to the nature spirits. If these beliefs seem particularly archaic in modern times, then we need look no further than the superstition of throwing money into water, which is still strong today. Rather than ancient wells in secluded communities being the focus for the old 'gift to the fairies' theme, the ornamental fountains in numerous modern Yorkshire shopping centres are overflowing with votive offerings! People still hold fast to the belief that they will be granted a wish when they toss pennies into the water, whether they would admit to believing in water spirits or not!

Eccleshall, in Sheffield, had fairy associations in the 19th century, when one of the oldest lanes (Dead Man's Lane) was rumoured to be a fairy dancing-place. Many rings of flowers and toadstools were prevalent here, traditionally associated with fairy circle-dances. The name 'Dead Man's Lane' is an example of the link between the dead and the fairy legend: there was a firm belief throughout Yorkshire, even into the 20th century, that fairies were the souls of the dead. Perhaps this offers an explanation for the belief that ancient burial sites were 'homes' of the fairies, although it does not explain why many ordinary folk believed that such souls resided in flowers! The foxglove and the broad-bean flower were particular favourites. Modern illustrated fairy-tale books still often show fairies appearing from the protective hood of harebells and foxgloves. This superstition is enhanced by the old Yorkshire belief that accidents are frequent when broad-beans are in flower, a superstition common to even the most practical of 19th century colliery workers. Unhallowed souls were said to be free to wander and create mischief when they escaped from broad-bean flowers!

The Fairy Death-Lantern

'When people are lost on the moors they sometimes see fairies dancing before them and leading them on their way...' S. O. Addy

The following story was recounted by Rotherham man Edward Law, who heard it from his father, a friend of the man it concerned. The name of this gentleman has been changed on request.

In the winter of 1947, weather conditions in South Yorkshire and North Nottinghamshire were so bad that a double decker bus had to be abandoned in the middle of its planned route. Within a few hours it was totally submerged underneath a drift of snow. It was one of the most severe winters in modern history.

During the ensuing blizzard, Whitwell man John Parker began to feel particularly concerned for the welfare of his elderly mother, who lived in Clowne. Against his better judgement, he decided to set off walking in the dark alone, hoping to reach her house later that night. He was concerned that if the old lady failed to light a fire, she could be left to freeze throughout the night.

Despite being wrapped warmly against the journey, it did not take long for Mr Parker to realise that he had made a dangerous decision. Blizzard conditions were making the journey particularly hazardous, and important landmarks had already disappeared into snowdrifts of several feet in depth. He became aware that if he lost his bearings, he would submit to the freezing conditions and succumb to hypothermia, possibly remaining undiscovered for long enough to literally freeze to death.

A side-effect of extreme cold is that it can produce hallucinations, and it was this that occurred to Mr Parker when he saw a glowing lantern appear in the darkness ahead of him, after he had been travelling for what seemed like several hours. Although the light was too far away for him to be able to distinguish any figure carrying it, he began to follow the glow as it moved away. (Mr Parker later noted that by this time, he had lost all feeling in his hands, feet and face due to the extreme cold.)

Eventually the lantern seemed to lead him to a point where the snow became more shallow underfoot... then it disappeared. At the point where it vanished, the shape of a row of houses became visible. Mr Parker struggled to reach his mother's front door. He entered the house, and found her lying on her death-bed. The source of the lantern remained a mystery to him, although he felt that it had not only heralded the death of his mother, but it had also very possibly saved his life.

Fairy Lights in Bleaklow

Bleaklow, in Derbyshire, is endowed with its own strange 'fairy lights' which appear and disappear unexpectedly and defy all logical explanation. On many occasions a powerful 'searchlight' beam has lit up whole areas of darkened countryside close to the Torside Reservoir, sending mountain rescue teams to search the lonely crags at night. On each occasion, they have returned empty-handed... and nobody has been reported missing. Other witnesses describe having seen 'a string of moving, elusive and eventually fading lights' on Bleaklow and the surrounding land.

The *Peak Park News* featured an eye-witness account of these strange lights in the early 1970's. A local school teacher was driving past the reservoir one night when 'the most brilliant blue light' lit up the terrain for miles around. As the witness drove into the light, she noted that, 'the air appeared to vibrate... [it] had the same brightness as lightning but this light lasted some three or four minutes... I asked around the neighbourhood but no one admitted seeing it and appeared reluctant even to discuss the matter.'

The following summer, the whole of Crowden Hostel was lit up by the same unidentified blue light, which seemed to emanate from the direction of Bleaklow. Rescue teams were called out to search the area, in case an emergency flare was responsible. However, the light continued to shine for over three minutes, and needless to say the rescue team eventually returned bewildered, having found no-one. On this occasion, the previous witness noted that many local people reluctantly admitted to having seen the light on several occasions before.

Fairy lights or fantasy? There is often a reluctance among witnesses to speak about strange and inexplicable phenomena such as this, as with the locals of Bleaklow. This fuels silent speculation as to the origin of such mystical lights, and legends of fairies and ghosts are continually reborn.

The Whitwell Fairy Tree

Late one night in the early 1970's, Jean Evans was driving home with her husband through Whitwell Common. Her attention was captured by what seemed to be several bright lights, or small fires, in a circle on the ground ahead of the car. As the vehicle moved closer, Mrs Evans was amazed to see a particularly ancient tree encircled by several fires which burned brightly around the base of its trunk. Not only this, but in the very centre of its branches, at some height, burned a further solitary fire. Unable to think what natural or even man-made phenomena could have caused such an unusual sight, Mrs Evans recalls feeling quite unnerved by the experience. Despite her curiosity, she had no intention of leaving the safety of the car to take a closer look!

Fairies have long been associated with ancient trees in their role as nature spirits. Did Jean Evans in fact see 'fairy fires', a form of unusual light associated with the fairy legend?

Witchcraft

The ancient and often misunderstood Wiccan religion has undergone a revival which has been recorded since the beginning of the century - and has most likely been happening for even longer. Modern witches hold fast to traditional beliefs which have roots in Celtic, Anglo-Saxon and Scandinavian culture, evident in this country long before Christianity was introduced. The witch-hunting mania of the 16th and 17th centuries was responsible for changing the image of the witch from that of the village wise-woman into the evil spell-caster. The modern revival of the 'craft of the wise' is more concerned with reinstating the true status of the traditional witch, although the very word itself often raises eyebrows among those who are unfamiliar with the traditional concept of witch-craft.

In pre-Christian times, each community would have held fast to certain festivals and beliefs and handed these down through the generations. Today, few modern witches can claim to have been born into the tradition of our forbears; rather, the witchcraft revival has re-adopted its old festivals and teaches them to new initiates. Religious persecution is probably the main factor in the disintegration of the old beliefs, although the Christian calendar itself has incorporated many pagan festivals into its own religious year: even the modern celebrations of Easter and Yuletide have their roots in pre-Christian religious festivals. Before the resurrection of Christ was adopted as a symbol of rebirth, Easter had been the festival of the Saxon Spring goddess Eostre, who also symbolised the coming of new life. Likewise, decking the halls with holly and ivy at Christmas-time harks back to pre-Christian days when these plants had their own mystical significance in the pagan religion.

Many pagan witches choose to exist rather anonymously, and do not go out of their way to recruit new members. Morgaine Bailey, a Sheffield-based Wiccan and coven leader, explained that a thorough screening process is undertaken whenever an interested party approaches her group with a view to joining. New members are never actively recruited, but those who look hard enough for an outlet for their beliefs will doubtless find a way of introduction. Any would-be member is met firstly on a social level, and then, if suitable, is invited into a 'pagan circle'.

Following this, as and when candidates are ready, they may be introduced into the practising coven as new initiates. Morgaine's Coven of Annis celebrate the old pagan festivals and acknowledge the existence of both God and Goddess. The religion is not anti-Christian, as those who fear the word 'witchcraft' often assume, but pre-Christian. The secrecy element of some Covens stems from the days when persecution of witches as 'devil worshippers' meant that it was safest to keep 'networking' to a minimum. Patricia Crowther, a well-respected South Yorkshire Wiccan who has been High Priestess of the Sheffield Coven for many years, said of her own group: 'We are not a secret society... just a society of secrets.'

Pagan Blessing

In 1990, Morgaine Bailey and a fellow Coven member were contacted by a distressed Sheffield resident who was experiencing unusual problems in her home. The woman in question lived in a large old stone-built house in Hillsborough, which had once been a butcher's shop. She had experienced unusual activity which seemed to indicate that her house was haunted. Strange atmospheres and spirit manifestations were disturbing the peace, and when an object was hurled at one of the children, it seemed that something had to be done. Morgaine and her colleague Anna visited the house in a bid to perform a 'banishing ritual', to persuade the 'presence' to leave, and pick up, if they could, an idea of its origin. As soon as they walked through the door, Morgaine remembers picking up the scent of 'frightened animals', although she was not aware at this time that the house had been a butcher's and that carcasses of many dead animals lay outside underneath several years' soil and turf deposits.

The witches informed the householder that they would need to visit every room, and proceeded on their tour with a candle, incense and water, to effect a blessing not totally dissimilar from the approach taken by the Christian Church. They started at the top of the house and worked their way down towards the cellar. Many rooms within the house had remained untouched by the family, and they were advised to 'reclaim' these by furnishing them with personal objects to give them a more 'lived-in' feel. One old fireplace in a small bedroom gave Morgaine the distinct feeling that deep within its base lay an unpleasant presence which was literally rising up from deep within the ground, into the house itself. She had an impression of ancient mineworkings which lay at its base, and a possible tragedy concerning the death of a child miner from some past period in history. The householder listened intrigued as Morgaine related her impressions, and confirmed that, somewhere underground in the vicinity of the house, there were indeed old mineworkings. The spirit of a young boy had also been seen by one of the children. Aside from this, Morgaine felt that within the house there remained the spirit of a young girl who had died in unhappy circumstances. Although the householder could not confirm this, a story told to me subsequently by another one-time resident of the same house suggests that this is likely to be accurate (see **Pagan Blessing in Hillsborough**).

When Morgaine and Anna visited the cellar, which had been used as a butchering area many years previously, they were greeted by an eerie sight - old stone slabs on which the carcasses would once have been prepared had been left in the huge room. Stone channels were cut into the floor for blood drainage, and the area was extremely cold and dark. The flame of the candle they were carrying began to retract despite there being no draught, and in one far corner, an ominous black shadow was visible. The two witches instantly located this, but continued calmly with the banishing ritual. Morgaine commented later that this shadow was most likely a culmination of the presences which were being banished. As though being swept up through the house, they were gathering in the last room to be visited, the cellar. The householder was advised (once again in common with the later story concerning the same house) that the spirit must not be 'invited' back, or it would be impossible to remove. With this in mind, the witches left, and the success of the ritual was never established, the house being sold shortly afterwards.

Morgaine Bailey's own house in Stannington is haunted by the ghost of its previous lady occupant. When she first bought the property it was fairly dilapidated, and needed renovation which meant that she could not live there for a time. On one occasion, Morgaine remembers arriving to decorate and leaving a roll of carpet at the foot of the stairs, which she later found had been turned around and laid neatly, even though there was nobody else in the house! The kettle often conveniently turned itself on at the wall just as she was thinking of making a cup of tea. When Morgaine first moved in, a friend lodged with her, and on one occasion had arrived back at the house just as Morgaine was preparing to set off for a late shift at work. Realising that she would be late, the friend offered to drive her to work, only to realise half way there that she had just put a pizza in the oven, and that it would be burnt to a crisp on her return. However, when she got back to the house the power socket at the wall was turned off... and the pizza was in the oven, perfectly cooked!

When Morgaine's daughter was a baby, her cradle was constantly rocked by an unseen hand. On several occasions when the baby became fretful in the night, an unknown hand turned on her little music box to soothe her.

The overall feeling that Morgaine has about the house is that her ghostly visitor wanted to see her old house 'settled in' again. Since renovations and gardening have restored the place to its former glory, the ghost has made its appearances less frequently. The presence is a friendly one, and when Morgaine recounted her tales to her neighbours who knew the previous occupant well, they were not surprised at the ghost's interest in the house - even from beyond the grave!

Clairvoyancy and Fortune Telling

'...sibyls or spae-wives, according to the popular fancy, went about the land and told men their fates. For this they received presents....' S. O. Addy

When the folklorist S. O. Addy travelled the North of England collecting folk and fairy-tales from people who had learned them from family members in time-honoured fashion, he stumbled across several with the central theme of witchcraft. In his own words: '...it will be seen that witchcraft is very prominent in our tales, and it will appear that gifts were made to witches to obtain their favour and assistance in the ordinary affairs of life.' This fascinating collection of Sheffield fairy-tales, with others from Derbyshire and North Nottinghamshire, is to be seen in Addy's book *Folk Tales and Superstitions*. Time and again folk-belief suggested that 'gifts ought to be offered to the witch, just as bowls of cream are offered to the fairies or local deities' .This may be reminiscent of seaside fortune-tellers who require that their palms be crossed with silver, but what of ordinary people who follow the old tradition of travelling the county telling fortunes?

In 1993, several inhabitants of Rotherham and Sheffield were approached (at various public houses, in shopping centres and so on) by an elderly lady who informed them that she was a clairvoyant. The lady refused all offers of payment, declaring that her gift was not to be used for monetary gain, but that she was merely 'sent to help' those with whom she came into contact. The messages she conveyed proved to be uncannily accurate for many of the people she spoke to, despite the woman having no previous knowledge of them.

Rotherham resident Mrs Liz Sendall was running a beauty salon on Percy Street at the time of the witch's visit, and remembers how an unassuming middle-aged woman walked into reception to book a treatment, and once on the couch proceeded to give her a clairvoyant reading! The witch informed Mrs Sendall that she too must have Romany blood, which was accurate since her great-grandmother had been a Spanish Romany gypsy. Details of family life and advice about situations which were soon to arise were described to Mrs Sendall which proved extremely accurate over the next few months.

The Norton Witch Tree

On Christmas Eve, 1891, the *Sheffield Telegraph* reported that, 'The last great gale blew down in the ground of Lightwood, Norton, a tree with a tradition. It is said to have been planted eighty years ago "to keep the witch out of the churn" [possibly connected with the belief that witches could prevent the churning of butter in a household they had "cursed"]... The people there spoke of the tree as the wiggin-tree.' The 'witch-wiggin' tree is another name for the mountain ash or rowan, long believed to have magical properties, including those of protecting innocent folk from black witchcraft. The Vicar of Wortley later added that the tree had been known to his parishioners as the Wickerberry Tree.

The Simmerdale Witch

A tale set in the old North Riding of Yorkshire, in a legendary sunken village known as Simmerdale, is that of the Simmerdale witch. Many years ago a witch is said to have visited this village, which had a church at one end and the house of a Quaker woman at the other. The witch travelled from door to door asking for food and drink, but at each and every house was refused and turned away. She eventually arrived at the house of the Quaker woman, where she was generously treated to meat, bread and beer. She had finished her meal while seated at the front step, then raised a twig of ash (presumably a magic wand) in the direction of the rest of the village, and chanted:

'Simmerdale, Simmerdale, Simmerdale sink,
Save the house of the woman who gave me to drink!'

whereupon the water level in the valley rose to monstrous proportions and swallowed every building except for the house of the Quaker woman. Villagers earlier on this century were convinced that, if they stared hard enough into Simmer Water, they could still see the ruins of the village and the church.

Clarkehouse Road: Site of a Coven?

In the Summer of 1994, workmen began renovating Lynwood House, an imposing listed building opposite the Royal Hallamshire Hospital on Clarkehouse Road in Broomhall, Sheffield. Lynwood was originally built for South Yorkshire businessman Henry Wilson Lofthouse around 1888, and was fortified during the Second World War when its cellar was made into an air-raid shelter with concrete walls nearly twenty inches thick. When it was purchased by the pub group Tom Cobleigh in early 1994, entry to the cellar of the building was only accessible through a solid steel door in the hillside. The workmen who broke through this

'The Horned God is the True God'

barricade were amazed to find a room 12 feet by 20 feet in size, which appeared not to have been touched for many years. Although a blazing hot day, the temperature in the cellar was noted at a mere eight degrees Celsius, and the workmen looked around in amazement to see a variety of what they assumed to be witchcraft symbols daubed on the walls. Letters later identified as those of the Theban alphabet (used by Wiccans) incribed a message on one wall, and on the floor was an enormous triple circle with a pentacle, the witches' five pointed star, in its centre. Another message reading 'The Horned God is the True God' was found on a vertical girder.

The workmen left the cellar in fear, and refused to return unless the place was exorcised, although several modern practitioners of the Wiccan religion assured the Tom Cobleigh Group that no evil was intended in the symbols. Beth Gurevitch, a Birmingham witch, said of the find: 'Wicca is a beautiful religion where karma is important to us. I think it is rather sad to wipe out a good presence... religious discrimination is silly in this day and age.' And local witch Morgaine Bailey, high priestess of the Stannington-based Coven of Annis, added: 'I am not convinced there is an evil presence in the house. All the signs indicate the coven worshipped a fertility god and goddess, so there's nothing to fear.'

The cellar was eventually blessed by a member of the Chesterfield Paranormal Research Bureau, Linda Hicklin, who commented afterwards: ' There's nothing to be frightened of; I've done a blessing and made it peaceful... if there had been anything down there, there would have been activity. Bricks would have been flying around, and people would have had accidents.' Whatever the intent of the inscriptions in the cellar, the new tenants can rest in peace that all has been done to ensure the building's future prosperity!

Altar at Nether Edge

In the early 1990's, South Yorkshire builder Steve Payne had been commissioned to modernise an old house in the Nether Edge area of Sheffield. This house, in common with many built in the last century, had a brick-built cellar which could be reached via a flight of steps. Mr Payne was given the key to the property, which was unoccupied at the time, and began to renovate it with a small team of employees. The men worked their way through the house and eventually reached the cellar, where they were intrigued to find that it still possessed, in its centre, an old stone slab table. The atmosphere here was somewhat chill, and on that particular day they were not reluctant to finish their shift and leave the house. Mr Payne locked up as normal; he noted that although the property needed improvement, it was in no way insecure, and there was no method of entry or exit to the cellar or any other part of the house, after the door had been locked at night.

The following morning the team returned to work, and entered the cellar to find a dead tortoiseshell cat lying on the stone slab table. The animal had obviously only recently died, and yet there had been no evidence of it the evening before. Mr Payne later noted that the most chilling thing was that the cat looked as though it had been stretched out intentionally on the stone slab. Although the builders generally thought of themselves as unsuperstitious and down-to-earth, they found themselves regarding the stone table as though it were some kind of altar, and the age-old superstition of black witchcraft, and animal sacrifice, reared its head once again...

The Haunted Cellar

Adrian Oakes is a South Yorkshire man in his late forties, but can still remember clearly an old house in the Nether Edge area of Sheffield where he lived as a small child. His family were plagued by what seemed to be poltergeist activity; objects would move around on their own, and strange atmospheres and noises were a regular occurrence during their short stay at the house, whose address has been withheld on request. Although the supernatural activity at the Oakes' Nether Edge home was frequent and varied, one particular episode which concerned Adrian's father Michael proved to be the most terrifying, and succeeded in forcing the family to leave soon afterwards.

Michael Oakes knew that the old basement cellar contained a large stone slab table, which he described as looking like an altar. He did not like the atmosphere in the cold damp room, and had never intended to use it. However, one evening he had gone down the cellar steps to fetch something, and must have blacked out, for the next thing he remembered was coming to half in a daze, lying on his back on the stone table. Mr Oakes could dimly picture several hazy figures standing around him as he lay on the table, and could hear vague and distant chanting. He felt as though he was fighting against something inexplicable, and was sure he was being held down. He eventually came round fully and ran out of the cellar in terror. Michael Oakes was not drunk or dreaming at the time of his experience. Needless to say, the family did not remain in the house for much longer. They were never able to find out any background history to the property, and can offer no explanation for the strange events which eventually drove them away.

The Creswell Crags Witch

The following story was recounted by a Rotherham man with an interest in the paranormal, who was involved in researching a strange event which occurred at Creswell Crags, near the South Yorkshire border. The Crags are a well-known cave formation around a natural lake, in which evidence of a Stone Age settlement has been found. They are now a protected site, and attract visitors from miles around, particularly during the summer months.

Towards the end of summer on a warm evening in the 1980s, a couple were driving home after an evening out when they halted at traffic lights at temporary roadworks, close to the Visitors Centre at the Crags. The passenger was resting her head against the window and trying to doze as her husband waited at a red light. Despite the weather being warm and the car being humid, she remembers feeling a sudden chill, which was also felt by her husband, who wound up the window on the driver's side.

As the couple waited for the lights to change to amber, the woman glanced out of the passenger window to her side. The sides of the road in this area are uncultivated, and bushes of briars and brambles grow densely underneath the trees. In fact, the briars were so thick at this point that they touched the side of the car. Less than two feet from where she sat, the woman caught sight of a pale, blurred circular shape around the size of a netball. It appeared to be suspended two feet off of the ground, caught on a thorny bush. She strained her eyes to see more clearly, unable to make out what it was, and reached for the handle to the car window to turn it down and take a better look. Before she had the chance, the shape began to float backwards and forwards as though it was being dangled on a string. All the while, it began to assume the features of what she later described as 'an old hag', with uncanny dark eyes and a beaked nose. Suspecting a practical joke by somebody hiding in the bushes, the woman remained sceptical as to what she was witnessing. However, the longer she observed the shape, the clearer it became. Distinctly feminine features were forming before her eyes, with hollowed cheeks and long dark hair below shoulder length framing a skeletal face. As the vision became clearer, the woman was convinced that she was witnessing a paranormal event. She later described the face as belonging to 'a witch' - in any case, the traditional version of what a witch supposedly looks like.

The vision formed in further detail, seeming pale, drawn and haggard, with warts and other skin blemishes and piercing 'hateful' eyes which the woman later described as being able to 'stare through' her. When the fully formed face, which had no evidence of a body attached to it, began to 'float' towards the car in which the couple sat, she screamed in terror. Her husband looked over to his left and saw, briefly, the eerie face for himself, before slamming the car into gear and racing off into the darkness.

Unfortunately, the incident proved so shocking to the young woman that on their arrival home, a doctor was called who prescribed her a sedative to calm her down. It was the doctor who persuaded the woman's husband to call the police, convinced that a dangerous prank had been played on the lonely country lane. A neighbour was called in to sit with his sedated wife while the man accompanied local police to the scene of the incident.

The police searched the area but were unable to find any clue as to what could have been responsible for the appearance of the mysterious head. One of the policemen even entered the thick brambles and thorn bushes at this point, to ascertain whether access would indeed have been possible for a practical joker. Entry was found to be almost impossible, and the policeman received cuts and scratches and ripped his uniform in the attempt.

Strangely, this was not the only sighting of something unusual to be reported in the area that night. Around dawn, a lorry driver was forced to brake hard and swerve to avoid a mysterious, dark figure which crossed the road from the Visitors Centre side at Creswell Crags. Thoroughly shaken by his encounter, he later described the figure as 'floating' and 'seemingly headless'. Instinctively, the lorry driver reported that the figure was female, although he had seen no face or other indication as to its sex. Once across the road, the cloaked figure disappeared into the thick bushes and vanished from sight.

Pagan Blessing in Hillsborough

It is very unusual to collect stories from different people who have at some point connected with the same haunted house, but this proved to be the case with an old house in Hillsborough, where totally by coincidence two separate witnesses who had not met were able to give their own stories about the same property. In the following story, names have been changed on request. Both accounts have the unusual distinction of involving a blessing by white witches as an attempt to lay to rest an earthbound spirit (see also **Pagan Blessing**).

In the autumn of 1990, Mark Jones and his girlfriend were preparing to move into a large stone-built house in Hillsborough, which had once been used as a butcher's shop. The family who were moving out were quite open about the fact that they believed the house to be haunted. Although the woman in question was convinced the presence within the house was friendly, her husband was not so forthcoming. She mentioned to the young couple that she had seen the ghost of a man in a white smock walk past her in the cellar, which had once been the area used for jointing meat when the house was run as a family butcher's.

Tales of the supernatural did not deter the new tenants, who moved in that winter. The house had no electricity at first, and was difficult to heat, having many rooms which were individually fitted with gas fires. The first strange occurrence took place one afternoon when Mark was in the house alone, waiting for his girlfriend to return from work. Aware of what the previous tenants had told him, he asked out loud that, if there were a presence in the house, would it make itself known, not expecting for a moment that anything would happen. He had turned the stereo up to full volume as he ran himself a bath, but as soon as he asked this question, it began to fade in and out every second or so at irregular intervals, leaving gaps of silence, although the record itself did not stop playing. This continued to happen for around fifteen seconds before resuming normal playing. Thoroughly frightened, Mark checked the stereo for faults but found none. The incident was never repeated.

The couple began to notice that in an evening as they sat in the living room, the smell of strong lavender would waft past them. This always happened at roughly the same time, and became a regular occurrence. The cellar area of the house, which still had meat hooks in place, had a particularly unpleasant atmosphere, and a visiting friend even refused to venture into it despite not having heard that the house may be haunted.

A little later, Mark's girlfriend walked into the bathroom to be startled by a towel moving quickly along the radiator as though caught in a strong draught, although the window was not open. Shortly before this, her daughter had been disturbed by voices which she had thought were calling to her from upstairs... although when she arrived, nobody was there.

When the couple had lived in the house for around six months, they were awakened one night by loud banging on their bedroom door. There was nobody outside the room; the burglar alarm at the top of the stairs had a beam which was intended to be triggered by intruders. Later they began to notice that the first person to go downstairs in the morning would find several lights on, which had certainly been turned off the night before. One particular morning, several of the gas fires in the house were turned on but not lit and were pouring out gas. Not long afterwards, curtains in the living room were found to have been opened first thing in the morning before anybody had entered the room.

Neither Mark nor his girlfriend ever really doubted that something strange was at work in the house, although they were resigned to tolerate it. Then one afternoon the couple began talking to a local woman. It emerged that this lady was a white witch, and conversation soon turned to the house in Hillsborough and the problems the couple had been encountering there. The witch was interested, and offered to visit with the promise that she could try to lay any 'presence' to rest.

It was drawing close the end of 1991, and the couple had been in the house for almost a year, when the white witch arrived one evening to look around for herself. Whether or not she had done any background research into the house was not clear, but she wandered around the rooms on her own before joining Mark and his girlfriend with a most unusual story.

The white witch felt that the spirit of a young girl who had died in the main bedroom was still earthbound. She identified this girl as the daughter to one of the early owners of the house, and suggested that she had died of anorexia. She also felt that the spirit was active in disrupting the relationships of any couple who lived there. The spirit was felt to be unhappy with any male presence in the house, but rather more supportive of the female! Mark remembered then how the couple who they had bought the house from had had disagreements as to the nature of the haunting. The woman felt the spirit to be friendly, whereas her husband had disagreed completely and felt that it was an aggressive presence.

The white witch planned to use a candle ritual to rid the house of the spirit, and chose the main bedroom, the room in which she felt that the girl had died many years before, as the place to perform this. She took a large white sheet with a five-pointed star on it, and lay an ornate glass candelabra at each corner. She lit four candles and warned the couple not to move them or put them out, but to allow them to burn the whole night through until they extinguished themselves. The couple slept in the room as normal that night, although they awoke twice; once to find that one of the heavy candleholders had tipped itself over and was setting the carpet alight, and the second time to find another candleholder split clean in two.

After the ritual, it was noticeable that the house, particularly the main bedroom, was warmer. The witch visited them to ensure that the ritual had been a success, although she was surprised that one of the candle holders had split, saying that nothing like that had happened before. She now felt that the girl's spirit had moved into the attic rather than disappeared completely, and said that it would not re-enter the main part of the house unless 'invited' to. Satisfied that the blessing had been at least in part successful, Mark Jones and his girlfriend decided to leave the area several months later, and the house remained empty until eventually sold.

Wizard casting out Devils

UFO's are not just a modern phenomenon: these spectacular black balls in the sky were seen over Basle, Switzerland, in 1566!

Unidentified Flying Objects

Unidentified lights in the sky, sightings of enormous, silent airborne machines, and 'V' shaped objects with brightly coloured lights whirring over housing estates at ridiculously low altitudes... the following selection of sightings were recorded in and around South Yorkshire. Many ordinary people who had never before encountered the unexplained, were suddenly contacting UFO research bureaux in droves. Most of the following accounts are previously unpublished, and go some way towards attempting to show the scale of the UFO wave which hit the North of England between 1987 and 1989.

Langsett Hill

Manchester man Larry Mayer had been visiting relatives in the Stocksbridge area of Sheffield, and was returning along the A616 at about 9.30 pm in September, 1987, when he came alongside a pine plantation and in his own words 'something inside me said "take your time"'. He slowed his car and in a clearing in the plantation, noticed 'several strips of light, alternate strips coloured red and white pulsating, first the red then the white and so on.' Mr Mayer felt that the lights gave the impression that they were attached to a circular object which was hovering some 50 feet off the ground, casting out enough light for the tips of the pine trees to be illuminated behind it. Interestingly, local police reported the appearance of strange lights in Stocksbridge itself around the same time as this witness reported his unusual sighting.

Barnsley

In early January 1988, Barnsley miner Carl Walker was on his way home from a night shift at Redbrook Colliery. Spotting a bright light above some trees towards the end of Huddersfield Road, he stopped his bike to observe further out of curiosity. Mr Walker watched in fascination as two 'bright lights' hovered side by side approximately 60 feet above the tree tops. Suddenly, a flashing red light appeared underneath the others and the object began to head in his direction, tilted at an angle. The terrified man stared into the object and felt that he could see a row of windows ('about eight or ten in all') at the top. Mr Walker remained frozen to the spot, but had the distinct feeling that 'whatever it was knew by some means that I was watching... I put my bike back into gear to drive away, but on doing so I glimpsed once more, where I noticed it tilt the same way I was going, the lights all went off, then it had just gone...' The object was roughly cross-shaped, and its underside was a metallic grey covered with 'boxes and machinery'. The witness had also been aware of 'a kind of eerie silence while the object was nearby' - something often described by people who have close encounters of this nature. Although Mr Walker was afraid to confide in too many people in case his story was scoffed at, he did feel strongly enough to contact the UFO investigative body BUFORA and was later interviewed in detail by visiting investigators. A mining colleague also commented that he too had seen a bright light in the sky as he left work that morning, but had thought no more of it. Exactly a month later, two witnesses in Rotherham described seeing a similar, large cross-shaped object flying silently at a low altitude over the Eastwood estate. Another local man managed to take photographs of an 'orange-yellow coloured light' after a UFO had disappeared over the horizon.

Thurnscoe

In September 1987, Houghton resident Sandra Taylor and her daughter witnessed an object 'as big as a dustbin lid' silently gliding over their heads in the small hours of the morning. It appeared to fly at a height of 100 feet, was triangular in shape, with an underside patterned with rows of white and orange lights. The object moved slowly towards some fields beyond the house before disappearing suddenly and quickly.

Longley Estate, Sheffield

A V-shaped object whirred past a psychology student one night in early October, 1987, as she walked along Holgate Crescent towards Holgate Road. The bright red lights, arranged in rows along its underside, were pulsating at different rates as it moved over the houses at only twice the height of the rooftops! Reports such as this one often prompt complaints to the Ministry of Defence about the dangers of low-flying aircraft... who usually deny that any of their craft were in the area at the time. Although a significant number of UFO's are reported to move silently through the sky, there were a number of eye-witness accounts at the time that match this one in its reference to a 'strange whirring noise' emanating from the object.

Chapeltown

Another report of a V-shaped object lit by red lights along its 'wings' came from a Sheffield woman on February 2nd, 1988, when almost twenty independent witnesses reported their sightings over the area to local UFO researchers. Local houses shook with the vibration of a 'strange whirring noise' as the object passed overhead, at an approximate altitude of 200 feet. At the same time, another Chapeltown resident was unloading shopping from her car when 'this large V-shaped thing passed over' with orange and red lights, sounding so strange that the witness imagined it to be a 'plane with engine trouble'.

Goldthorpe

Rotherham security guard Derrick Anders reported to the *South Yorkshire Times* how he had seen a triangular object with orange and white lights 'jetting silently across the sky' on New Year's Eve in 1987. Mr Anders was 'not a believer in UFO's', but out of curiosity had his telephone number printed in the South Yorkshire Times asking any other witnesses to come forward and contact him. Consequently, he received over thirty telephone calls from local people who had seen a triangular object with coloured lights arranged in a V shape 'just like a snooker diamond', travelling slowly enough for observers to get a clear description before it jetted out of sight.

Rotherham

In early January 1988, *Quest* magazine reported two local men as having witnessed 'a cluster of brilliant glowing yellow and red coloured lights' above their heads at an altitude of approximately 750 feet, in the Masborough area. Later in the same evening, Kimberworth man James Clark told how he saw 'a large glowing orange/yellow ball of light moving extremely slowly' in a north-westerly direction. These sightings were followed with less-detailed accounts of 'lights in the sky' throughout the area, many of which possibly had rational explanations. A local newspaper reported that 'three individual unidentified targets followed by military aircraft were seen flying above a residential area.' Other reports on the same night record that various unusual formations of coloured lights were spotted in the sky, and a 'Flying Complaint Form' was filed by a Rotherham UFOlogist to the Ministry of Defence in London. The Ministry, however, denied that increased flying activity had taken place in the area.

Shiregreen, Sheffield

Sheffield local historian Peter Smith reported an interesting sighting in February 1988, which he recorded whilst sitting at his desk and looking out of the window. First attracted by a strange noise, Mr Smith glanced up and saw an object resembling a 'pudding basin' which seemed to be travelling at great speed and climbing in altitude all the time. The object was dark, but was partly illuminated by two very bright crimson red lights. It disappeared over the horizon within five seconds, and the witness described the sound it made as 'a cross between a heavily-burdened diesel engine and the sound that the little flying saucer makes in the Arcade game "Space Invaders"'.

Broomhill, Barnsley

In April 1988, around 9.45 pm, Mrs Linda Sage and her daughter were surprised to encounter a large elliptical object with red, green and white flashing lights around its outline, hovering soundlessly over the road between Broomhill and Wombwell. Both witnesses noted that the area was strangely quiet as it hung in the air, remarking how this was unusual as the road was normally a busy one. When they observed the object, which was about 'the height of two houses' above them, it appeared to switch on two white spotlights which lit them up clearly. They had the feeling that they were being watched, and as the daughter urged her mother to carry on walking as though they had not noticed it, the spotlights went out. Mrs Sage had the feeling that the object had somehow 'spotted' them and turned a full circle in the air to shine spotlights on them both. Approximately ten minutes after their first sighting of the UFO, it raised itself into the night sky and disappeared. The next day, other local people testified to having seen mysterious lights in the sky at the same time as Mrs Sage and her daughter had their close encounter.

Cantley, Doncaster

Two residents of Cantley, north-east of Doncaster, witnessed a brilliant white light similar to a 'quartz halogen lamp' hovering above the chimney pots of houses close to Hawthorn School. With a clear view from their patio window, they watched for a quarter of an hour as the glowing white ball lit up playing fields from its stationary position. One of the witnesses described how 'the light came from all round it and down at the bottom like a helicopter searchlight.' As no markings on the object were clear, the witnesses decided to fetch a pair of binoculars. However, the glow emitted was so intense that the glare effect through the lens meant that they could not distinguish anything further. The object appeared on two further occasions, and was seen by another member of the family who decided to leave the house to investigate further. Upon leaving the house to approach it, the glowing light 'went like a red glow and disappeared.' RAF Finningley were contacted and asked whether the light in the sky could possibly have been one of their aircraft, to which they replied that it was not. The sightings were not confined to this particular family alone, and several newspapers, both regional and national, showed an interest in the story. The case was subsequently researched by the Direct Investigation Group of Aerial Phenomena and the Independent UFO Network in some detail. No firm conclusions were ever drawn.

Carlton, Barnsley

In early 1988 a Barnsley miner was astounded to look into the sky and see what he at first thought to be a communications satellite with solar panels... until he realised that its altitude was much too low! Ruling out the possibility of an aeroplane, since it was not moving, the startled miner continued to observe and make a mental note of its details. The object seemed to be 'three times the size of a jumbo jet', and hovered around the altitude of 600 feet. Its body was of an aluminium colour, and its underside featured a large cross-shape of panels. Around its edge were flickering 'portholes'. In the words of the witness: 'I watched it for a few minutes and noticed that it was tilting - the full cross was visible and then only part of it when it tilted towards me and I could see a small dome on top of it... the round portholes were of less density and flickered.' The man continued to watch the object for a further quarter of an hour before entering Carlton Club.

Wombwell, Barnsley

A woman walking home one evening had almost reached her gate when she was alerted by an unusual droning noise which gradually got louder. For a moment she thought that a low-flying 'plane must be responsible, although if so it sounded dangerously close to the housing estate. She looked up into the sky to see which direction it was flying from, and in her own words, 'realised it was coming from inside the cul-de-sac, just above the roof-tops. I could not see what the shape was, it looked like a big black mass, especially with the sky being very black as well, but all the lights underneath it were very bright red and silver... I knew at once that it definitely wasn't a 'plane - I knew it was something very unusual.' The object began to climb steadily, and only its lights remained visible. It started to move off in the direction of Hoyland, where more witnesses saw it. A man sitting in his car saw the same object appear over the rooftops, at an altitude of around 200 feet, travelling towards Hoyland. He described it as 'diamond- or pyramid-shaped', having five sides to its body which 'was surrounded by a mass of lights of many different colours', and making a whirring noise as it slowly moved onwards. A group of people in a car close to where this witness was parked also appeared to be watching the same unusual sight. After several minutes the object disappeared from view, and from here the story was continued by witnesses from Hoyland, as it hovered over one particular street for five minutes keeping several observers spellbound!

The North Nottinghamshire Sightings

The following story was recorded by an 'unexplained' enthusiast from the Rotherham area, who compiled the following accounts from first-hand witnesses of unidentified flying objects. All names have been changed on request, although the locations remain the same.

In the early 1980's, motorist John Field was startled by a fiery light crossing his path from left to right, one morning as he drove close to Creswell Crags, just outside South Yorkshire. The object blazed out of view, heading in the direction of Whitwell. This sighting could easily have been an example of natural astronomical phenomena, such as a meteorite, and if the story had not been reported, then local police would not have begun a catalogue of similar sightings which were soon to escalate in a most unexpected way.

David Anderson and Paul Baker were walking across Bakestone Moor early that same morning, heading for Creswell, when they spotted an orange ball of fire in the sky. It seemed to be on course to hit a row of houses nearby, until it crashed into a recently ploughed field several yards away, landing silently. Unbeknown to both men, who agreed on mutual silence as to what they had witnessed, a woman standing at her bedroom window in one of the nearby houses had also seen the 'light' land in the field. June Emery had seen an 'orange ball of light' descending with great speed from the sky, which she described as a 'metallic sphere the size of a bucket' which was engulfed in orange flames. As the object landed, Mrs Emery noted that it not only made no sound, but it also left no impression on the earth in the field which it impacted. Later that same day, Paul Baker visited the field near to Bakestone Moor in an attempt to see whether any evidence of his previous sighting had come to light. He, too, saw that the field was undisturbed, and drew no response from a local shopkeeper in an attempt to find out whether any other locals had seen and reported the incident. That evening, June Emery, after initially spotting the mysterious object from her bedroom window, was surprised to see two policemen searching the spot at which it had 'crashed'. Both policeman were carrying torches and wearing wellingtons, and one of them carried a large stick which he used to probe into the soil. Twice he passed over the very spot at which Mrs Emery had seen the mystery object sink into the earth. She watched as the men, finding nothing, left the scene.

That night, two young people from Clowne (who were not acquainted) were standing at a bus stop in town when the young woman

103

felt overcome by a 'sensation of sudden quiet'; she later described this as 'sending a chill down her spine'. Feeling a sudden compulsion to look up above her head, she was amazed to see an enormous mass of dark metal riddled with pipes and valves, which seemed to float swiftly and silently over the street at roof-top height. Several seconds after the object disappeared from view, the young man also present turned and asked if she was alright... before disappearing into the night, having obviously witnessed the same thing for himself.

At about the same time, Dave Evans was walking his dog on Gapsick Lane at the eastern end of Clowne close to the electricity sub-station, when the animal suddenly bolted towards home. Mr Evans could see no obvious reason for his pet's behaviour, although he did notice a greenish light which seemed to envelop the sub-station, but thought at the time that this was a natural phenomenon which occurred occasionally on certain foggy nights... until he realised that the night was clear! It was at this point that Mr Evans glanced upwards and saw a huge dark shape moving slowly across the night sky in the direction of Bakestone Moor.

Within the same hour, two Whitwell women, a mother and daughter, had taken the youngest woman's little girl to the local recreation ground, which was clearly lit by streetlamps. All three stood in fascination and stared towards a row of houses a few hundred yards away, where a huge, dark circular object with a ring of multi-coloured flashing lights around its base was slowly drawing towards them. The underside of the object soon covered the whole of the recreation ground, and it was only then that they realised its extreme size. Strangely, nobody present on this particular occasion felt any fear or apprehension; rather, they felt as though they were honoured to have witnessed such an event. However, both women decided to err on the side of caution and, once the object had begun to move away in the direction of Worksop, they advised the little girl that this must be 'their secret'.

Half a mile from the recreation ground, Iris and Peter Sanders were walking to visit relatives when the street lamps suddenly dimmed and flickered out. They glanced towards the nearby houses and noticed that these, too, had suffered a power cut. However, the entire street was not affected - a group of houses all in close proximity were the only ones in darkness. As they continued to walk, the couple noticed with surprise that this had occurred on several other streets, with only certain houses on each road affected. In each case, the power cuts lasted no more than twenty minutes. When the lights came back on, they appeared weak at first, before resuming normal brightness.

Shortly afterwards, local police received several telephone calls from people in the Manton Colliery area who had spotted a bright light hovering overhead. Hours later, a local couple and their friends were preparing to say goodnight when they looked out into the darkness and saw a host of bright lights darting about in the sky, in the direction of Bolsover. This continued for several minutes.

Despite numerous investigations, no object was ever found in the field at Bakestone Moor. Local newspapers reported the sighting of a UFO over Manton Colliery, and that same week there were several reported sightings of UFO's in the nearby Peak District. When all the reported sightings and other related incidents were plotted on a map, it was found that they formed a straight line.

Rational Explanations?

Aircraft bases throughout the country run test-flights of which a number are likely to involve an element of 'secret' testing, whether it concerns new forms of aircraft or unusual flightpaths. Astronomical phenomena, such as starlight 'magnified' by unusual weather conditions, or the passage of comets close enough to the earth's atmosphere to be detected by the human eye, could also be held responsible. There are also cases of misguided witnesses who have held binoculars or telescopes to particularly bright stars, which they have then reported as 'moving lights' - when in actual fact, any slight shaking of the hand can make a stationary object appear to have its own 'irregular flight-path'! UFO 'abduction' stories have always created headline sensations and titillated the curiosity of a general public who profess not to believe in such things, and yet if the popular press is to be believed, still cannot read enough about them!

But, for those who do not believe in Unidentified Flying Objects, the last word must go a Sheffield policeman who was interviewed in the late 1980's by the Independent UFO Network: 'Most of the lads I used to work with at Ecclesfield have seen strange lights over Greno Woods. A lot of people at Deepcar, nightwatchmen, and security guards at Oughtibridge have seen them coming over Wharncliffe Woods. The one that sticks in my mind the most was in the early 1980's, when everyone on the night shift saw a huge blue saucer-shaped thing like a huge blue sheet of steel going across the sky.' Apparently, police in the area rarely report their observations to the RAF or MOD: 'Our people see so many weird things on the night patrol that it's not worth it...'

Norton Church

Historic Sites and Haunted Halls

The following selection of historic locations possess everything from Grey Ladies and phantom monks, to ghostly rattling chains and hidden graves. Most of these places can be visited by the general public, and many have fascinating histories which are just as colourful as the rumours of their supernatural guests...

Conisbrough Castle

The picturesque Conisbrough area of Doncaster was once known as 'Conyngeburg', Old English for 'King's Borough', possibly stemming from the time when this area of South Yorkshire was part of the ancient kingdom of the Northumbrian royals. Conisbrough has certainly seen its fair share of change in rulership over the centuries, and has been mentioned by Chroniclers Geoffrey of Monmouth (who referred to it as Caer Conan) and Bede, among others.

A 13th century Chronicle describes the visit of King Egbert and his retainers to the court one Whitsuntide:

> 'Sone after the wyntere, whan the somer bigan,
> The Kyng and his meyne went to Burgh-Konan.
> It was on Witsonday.'

The Romans named Doncaster Danum, after a pagan goddess, and set up fortified camps throughout. The Normans took possession after the Conquest, and usurped the previous Saxon lords. Domesday records show that Conisbrough belonged to Earl William de Warenne, who was son-in-law to the Conqueror himself. It is unknown whether the rise of land on which the Castle is built is natural or man-made, although whatever its origin, it is likely to have been used by each new conquering people as a fortified mount.

In 1989, a family wedding photograph was taken in the ancient St Peter's Churchyard, close to the Castle, parts of which date back to 900 AD. A young pageboy had posed for a snapshot on which only he was visible to the photographer... until the print was developed, revealing the shadowy shape of a woman in the background holding what appeared to be a small baby.

Historic Lower Sprotborough, near Conisbrough, is close to the ancient Roman Doncaster road. Rich with history, it is also graced by an ancient cottage which is reputed to have been used by Sir Walter Scott when writing his famous novel *Ivanhoe*, set at Conisbrough Castle. When Ian Thompson was offered the post of General Development Manager of the Castle on behalf of the Ivanhoe Trust, in 1994, he and his wife Annabel moved into this very cottage. They were delighted with its seclusion as well as its historic connections,but soon began to report small personal objects disappearing and doors being opened and closed.

Unconcerned although puzzled, the couple have catalogued many unusual disturbances in the cottage, not least of all when Ian left his seat one evening and returned moments later to find it covered with huge chunks of coal! Stranger still, Annabel had been sitting in the chair next to his all the time and had noticed nothing amiss... one moment the chair was empty, and the next, inexplicably, it was covered with coal.

Two well-known ghostly tales concerning this area are those of the Grey Monk and the White Lady. The phantom monk has been spotted in and around the Castle over a period spanning several hundred years. On 7 July 1778, Richard Glafsby of Yorkshire returned home from a visit to Conisbrough Castle and recorded in his journals: 'On the night before today, in Castle built of Cunisbro' stone myne eyes have seen Phantom of Abbot Monk alowne. In the castle with a candel lyt, he wos only in castel chapel wore he dyd not syt. Ome at Mecesboro, Bettey my wife I towld of the Phantom and she spowk, "No mower must you spake naw of them fantommy fowk." I was cauld, caulder than fust man thut deed and scayed, but I be not scayed or could no mower. O Pray for the cursed Cunisbro' Abbot Monk, that wrought this hour to me! May the Lord take pity on hym, and take me wen I dee...'

In 1830 it was the turn of Conisbrough residents Alexander Slidell and Eve Effingham, who saw the spectre of a grey monk in the castle grounds. Thirty years later Richard Maclehouse added his sighting to theirs, and in 1940, the Wesleyan Methodist Rev. Hutchins spotted the monk in the Castle.

The White Lady was said to have been the wife of one of the many lords of the Castle, who was pushed to her death over the edge of the donjon (tower) when her husband discovered that she was having an affair. Ever since, her pale shade has been condemned to haunt the ruins.

The eyecatching Norman tower of Conisbrough Castle, visible for many miles around, is one of the finest examples of its kind in Europe. Constructed at the end of the 12th century by Earl Hamelin Plantagenet, the tower is believed to have once been whitewashed. Lit to blinding whiteness by the sunlight, the 93 foot high structure would have stood out over its rural surroundings as the ultimate symbol of the conquerors' power. Today, the tower looks surprisingly modern alongside the remaining crumbling walls of Conisbrough Castle. Built from magnesium limestone, it is self-cleaning, and although the interior did not survive as well, recent renovations have now restored its former glory.

The Grave of Hengist, a mound of earth on the inside of the Castle walls, marks the spot where this ancient Saxon warrior is reputed to be buried. Although it seems unlikely to be any more than a local legend, excavations are not possible because of the situation of the site. According to various versions of the legend which have been recorded by chroniclers over the centuries, Aurelius Ambrosius (elected King of the Britons) fought the Saxon King Hengist in a local field, defeating him. Hengist ran to the castle at 'Caerconan' in a vain attempt to escape, but Ambrosius pursued and captured him, marching the Saxon outside the city walls before beheading him. Reputedly a gentle man, Ambrosius then made sure that Hengist was buried according to the traditions of his own people, in a Pagan barrow ... which today can be seen as a grassy hillock close to the visitors' centre.

Late at night in early October 1994, Doncaster police were called to investigate a break-in at Conisbrough castle. It was not the old Norman tower which had been the target of their attentions; rather, a small storage unit just inside the main wall had been forced with a crowbar. At the time, the tower interior was undergoing renovation, and the electricity supply had not been connected. The lighting inside the castle tower was provided by a generator which was only switched on by the builders each morning.

When the police arrived, they pointed out a lit window in the tower to General Development Manager Ian Thompson, who was as mystified as they were as to its origin. The light appeared to be emanating from a small window which was once the tower Chapel, and indeed, many local people have seen a mysterious glow coming from the same window late at night, when the premises are supposedly empty and locked to the outside world. Could the phantom Chapel light have any connection with Richard Glafsby's sighting of a ghostly monk holding a candle in the same room, over two hundred years before?

The building team themselves were troubled by a 'cold spot' in the lower portion of the tower, which is home to a deep and eerie well, a place reputed to host an atmosphere of evil. Strange whisperings have been heard on the stairwell, and unexplained voices occasionally shout out incoherent words from unoccupied floors of the building. A party of school children were on a guided tour in 1994 when their attention was attracted by loud tapping from the floor above. The tour guide hesitated before commenting that the builders must be at work on the upper floor... only to be surprised by the appearance of a builder behind him who remarked that no work was being undertaken at that time!

One local of Conisbrough, who does not wish to be named, gave the following story in an attempt to explain the mysterious presence in the tower. The tower is reputed to be haunted by the Countess of Cambridge, who died there in 1446. During her lifetime, she would often have frequented the Earl's room on the first floor, which sports a magnificent fireplace and was used for state meetings and the entertainment of visiting dignitaries.

The lady who recounted this story had felt a 'presence' in the room on several occasions, and as she was keen on meditation and relaxation techniques, she decided to utilise her skills in an attempt to 'contact' the Countess. Rather than doing this in the Castle Tower itself, she was at home one morning in bed when she cast her mind to the Earl's room in an attempt to make contact. The lady described how a vision of a fair haired woman in a long blue dress and blue hat appeared to her, standing by the ladies' seats next to the small window. She commented on the vision's fair hair and beauty, and the fact that the woman appeared to be in her prime. In her waking dream state, the lady then informed the Countess that she knew she could see her, but could she possibly make her presence felt to one of the members of staff at the Castle (a friend) by means of an agreed 'sign'. The vision of the Countess made the signal of three loud and slow raps on a wooden panel, and the 'dream' was over.

Later during the same day, the lady's friend reported hearing three loud slow raps emanating from an unoccupied area of the tower while he was in there alone... despite having no previous knowledge of her waking dream. Indeed, it was only after he reported this to her that she went physically pale and told him of her strange experience that morning! With the initial shock over, the lady commented that the overall feeling she was left with from her contact with the Countess was one of happiness. The Countess appeared to be delighted that the tower, her former home, was being renovated to its former splendour, instead of remaining an empty shell as it had done for many years.

In June 1995 an all-night vigil was undertaken at the Castle by a team of thirteen researchers from PARA-SEARCH, ASSAP [The Association for the Scientific Study of Anomalous Phenomena], and the Sheffield Paranormal Research Group. A video camera was trained on the Chapel (the sight of phantom lights on many occasions), electronic thermometers were placed throughout the building to ascertain whether any cold-spots developed, and tape recorders were left on each of the three floors of the donjon. Trip-wires were also set up in an area only known to one of the groups, to eliminate human tampering if any unexplained phenomena were to occur. The team split into three groups which kept notes of sights and sounds occurring throughout the night, changing their location every few hours.

The vigil was not particularly productive; the only odd happening occurred at around 3 am in the morning, when one of the upper doors slammed suddenly despite there being no wind. Several of the observers also noted the unexpected sound of running water, which proved impossible to locate and was never satisfactorily explained. Several earlier vigils in the donjon had also failed to produce any substantial results, although doubtless there will be more research groups in the future who are willing to spend the night at the Castle waiting for the supernatural to happen!

The White Lady of Clifton Hall

In the late 1970's, the *Rotherham Advertiser* ran a column for local people who had had supernatural experiences, inviting them to come forward and tell their tales. One elderly Rotherham resident, Mrs Nettleship, recounted an episode which concerned her family, and had taken place in a house on Clifton Lane, Rotherham, in the mid-1930's.

The Nettleships had two young children, baby Roy and four-year-old Audrey, and their circumstances meant that the whole family were forced share the same bedroom. A fortnight after moving into their new home, the little girl began to grow fretful when left in the bedroom alone, and insisted that a 'white lady who shook her hands and cried' was appearing as she lay in bed. Putting this down to the vivid imagination of a child, the Nettleships reassured Audrey that nobody could get into the bedroom, and assumed she had been dreaming.

Several months later, Mrs Nettleship discovered an old-fashioned doll in a cardboard box in the bedroom, which had previously lain hidden on a high shelf. As the family were poor, she decided to keep the find a secret and repair the doll as a Christmas present for Audrey. She returned the doll to its box and replaced it on the shelf. It was shortly after this discovery that, at around 9.30 pm one evening, the Nettleships were in the living room when they were startled to hear screaming coming from the bedroom. They ran in to find Audrey in a state of shock, such that her mother later described her as 'rigid with terror'. Mrs Nettleship noticed that Audrey's nightdress was torn, and took the little girl downstairs to comfort her.

Audrey described how the 'white lady' had tried to 'take her away', and she had had to fight to pull away from her. Although the Nettleships could see for themselves that their daughter was in a terrible state, they dismissed the story as a vivid nightmare. However, as time progressed, Audrey became more and more subdued, stopped eating and eventually became ill. Mrs Nettleship took her to the childrens' clinic, and the doctor informed her that somebody or something was obviously frightening the little girl very badly for her to be in such a state of terror. The Nettleships once again put this down to the 'nightmares' which they assumed Audrey had been having, since their baby son Roy (who slept in a cot next to her) had never once been disturbed in the night.

Shortly afterwards, the family decided to move house, but before they left, Mrs Nettleship went to look for the old doll she had found some months previously in the bedroom. The box was exactly where it had always been, but the doll had vanished. Nobody else admitted to having even seen it, and in its position on the high shelf it would have been very difficult for Audrey herself to have removed it.

Although the happenings on Clifton Lane were never quite forgotten, the family continued with their new life in a different area of Rotherham and soon the memories faded into the past. Then, many years later, an article in the *Rotherham Advertiser* caught Mrs Nettleship's eye. In a piece about local ghosts, The White Lady of Clifton Hall was mentioned. As she cast her mind back to the old house on Clifton Lane, where Audrey had experienced such discomfort as a child, Mrs Nettleship was horrified to read that the self-same White Lady is said to appear wringing her hands in distress as she cries for her lost children... and began to believe for the first time that perhaps somebody - or something - could have indeed tried to take her small daughter away.

Wentworth Woodhouse and Lady Mabel College

The site of this Jacobean mansion was the family seat of the Wentworths from the 1400's onwards. The house is mentioned twice in the *Guinness Book of Records*; once as the largest house in England, and secondly as the house with the longest frontage. After the house became a college, students reported on many occasions feeling as though they were 'being watched', and several of the unluckier ones among them even felt the sensation of being 'prevented' from climbing the stairs by an invisible force!

Thomas Wentworth resided in the Hall at the time of King Charles I, acting as administrator to the royal family, until he was beheaded for political treachery. His ghost was believed to appear at 11.00 pm each night walking down the stairs from the oldest part of the mansion, where his living accommodation was once situated. Another spectre at the Hall is an unknown female spirit, rumoured to be a member of the Rockingham family, who allegedly had an affair with a footman to the disgrace of her family. After her death she continued to appear at the end of Chapel Corridor, close to the old servants' quarters where she would once have walked by dead of night to engage in secret trysts with her lover.

Despite the history of the Hall, many people who have resided there have described its atmosphere as 'friendly' and 'lived-in', and an all-night vigil by ghost-hunters in the 1970's turned up no new leads, despite the fact that Thomas Wentworth's ghost was expected to appear at its usual time of 11 o' clock!

The Forgotten Grave

When Bassetlaw General Hospital was under construction, workers preparing the foundations uncovered what they at first took to be the bones of a prehistoric animal, along with many ancient human skeletons who all had broken necks. The remains were sent to archaeological specialists at the Creswell Crags Centre, which was established after the discovery of a Stone Age settlement there. After many tests, it was revealed that the large bones were the jaws of a giant whale, and the skeletons were possibly victims of a gibbet from the same site. Archaeological experts felt that the entrance to the mass-graveyard had once been marked by the upstanding whale bones, which had fallen with the passage of time and become buried.

North Nottinghamshire local historian Ernest Baker was called out to repair the radar on an 'Ack-Ack' site near Tickler's Hill, Tickhill, during the War. Gallows Hill revealed a bone structure of similar proportions to the one found in the Bassetlaw Hospital foundations, and although no skeletons were forthcoming, Mr Baker noted that his brief had told him to expect the presence of ancient remains in the area. Whatever was once preserved there is now forgotten, part of an ancient culture removed by the expansion of our own.

Haworth Hall

The mid-1960's saw the demolition of a beautiful historic house which had for 340 years stood in the Canklow Meadows area of Rotherham. Haworth Hall, seat of the Haworth family for several generations, had a haunted reputation which lives on to this day in the memories of all those who knew it.

In Elizabethan times, daughter of the house Elaine Haworth was brutally murdered by her jealous suitor Sir Herbert Vayne, who was then tried and sent to his death at York City gallows for the crime. After her death, residents of the Hall spanning several generations told of heavy footsteps and the rustle of long gowns echoing from many of the old, dark rooms which existed on the second floor of the building.

At the beginning of the 18th century, one of the house's occupants discovered a secret room behind one of the large fireplaces in the dining room. It was fully furnished, including a large bed on which the curious investigator was horrified to find a skeleton... believed to be that of William Haworth, the brother of murdered Elaine. The story of his death remains a mystery; the location of the secret room must only have been known to a select few at the time of his disappearance - until his body was stumbled across by accident, many years later.

There is a strange echo here of the much better-known story of Minster Lovell Hall, in Oxfordshire, where Francis Lovell is reputed to have fled for safety after the battle of Stoke, secreting himself in a hidden room whose whereabouts was known only to an aged and trusty servant. The retainer unfortunately died that very night, leaving Lovell to perish of starvation, only being rediscovered in 1708 when workmen making alterations broke unexpectedly into the room, seeing a skeleton in rags, seated at a table over an open book, all of which, rags, books, skeleton, and table, faded to dust with the inrush of air, before their very eyes. The two stories are so similar, perhaps they are both versions of an earlier, now lost, occurrence?

The Grey Lady of Aston Rectory

The Sheffield village of Aston has many ancient buildings and several local legends and hauntings associated with these, including tales of murder in the old Aston Hall, and rumours of secret underground tunnels said to riddle the terrain. The old Aston Rectory supposedly housed the spirit of a mysterious Grey Lady in period costume (whose identity is open to dispute) who would glide along in crinolines, and is even reported to have spoken to two women in the 1900's and introduced herself as Dorothy! The site of the building is thought to have foundations of over 600 years in age, although most of the later Rectory was designed by the noted architect John Carr in the late 1700's.

Local resident Mrs Eleanor Gorka spotted the Grey Lady for herself, standing at her bedroom window and looking down over the garden. She described her as young and slim, and, of course, dressed in grey. After this sighting, another three people came forward independently to report having seen the same spectre in broad daylight.

Local legend has it that Dorothy was either a daughter of the house or a maidservant, who was murdered by a footman (possibly her lover) and haunted the place thereafter. Her footsteps were often heard crossing the landing at 6 o'clock precisely each evening. When Dorothy appeared to two local women earlier this century and introduced herself, she informed them that they would be able to verify her existence by searching for her name in the parish register, and gave the year under which they should look. The women duly checked and found that their ghost's name was indeed recorded in the parish register, and so the woman had existed.

Black stains on the back stairs of the Rectory were said to be remnants of the fateful night Dorothy was murdered, as her blood had seeped into the floorboards and could not be removed. Ever since, Dorothy's appearance has been regarded as an ill-omen.

115

It is alleged that an exorcism once took place at Aston Rectory, presumably to rid the building of Dorothy's presence. The medium involved claimed that the spirit of Dorothy was about to reveal the location of hidden treasure... in great excitement, a small party searched the spot, but found nothing there. Dorothy obviously had the last laugh!

Norton Church

Whether or not there are any modern witnesses to supernatural activity in Norton Church, Sheffield, is unknown, although an interesting tale was recorded by the folklorist S. O. Addy concerning a strange event which took place in the last century:

'About 1840 the parish clerk of Norton and his apprentice went to play the organ, then standing in the west gallery of the church. The apprentice, whose face was turned towards the nave of the church, told the clerk that he could see a woman sitting alone in one of the high cloth-covered pews, and that he believed she was spectral. Thereupon they both rushed frantically down the steps, which were very tortuous and awkward. The clerk would never again play the organ in church in the dusk of evening.'

Bowshaw House and Farm

This rambling Georgian farmhouse hall, in the Bowshaw area of Dronfield, was built in the early 1730's by the locally influential Lucas family, a name still associated with the iron and steel business in the area. Despite its handsome proportions, Bowshaw was never considered to be a house of consequence at the time of its building, and is situated on the outskirts of Dronfield town centre.

In common with many other properties of such an age, Bowshaw has been updated and altered over the centuries, not least of all in the 1940's when a family feud split the property in two. Then owned by the Hatfield family, it was inherited by two brothers who could not decide how to divide the house and lands between them. Up until this point, Bowshaw House had been a large 'U' shaped building with a grand portico entrance. The only solution to the feud seemed to be splitting the house into two separate parts, which became known as Bowshaw House and Bowshaw Farm respectively. A wall was constructed in the old farm-house kitchen, which split the property, leaving Bowshaw House the portico entrance and a large garden, whilst enabling Bowshaw Farm to continue as a working farm with a separate entrance and several acres more land.

The House and Farm have passed through many hands throughout their history; Arthur Lee of the well-known local steel business bought the House to renovate in the 1950's, and then in the 1970's, it was taken over by its current owners, Jean and Keith Rowlinson.

Jean was told by an ex-gardener to the House, who was in his eighties, that there had always been rumours of underground tunnels which ran from the cellar of the house to Dronfield Parish Church, about half a mile away. The Green Dragon, a pub opposite Dronfield Church, boasts rumours of a similar underground passage. It therefore came as a surprise to Jean when, as she was leafing through the local *Star* newspaper one evening, she came across a scrap of archaic local history which noted that whoever lived at Bowshaw House had the right to a pew at Dronfield Church!

When the Rowlinsons decided to decorate the cellar as a play room for their two children, they found a large proportion of it had been blocked off and bricked up by previous residents. Although curious as to the legend of the secret tunnels, the Rowlinsons decided against opening up any of the plastered areas, and opted instead to re-lay the cellar floor, and install radiators and lights to make it more accessible. The cellar had never been a particularly damp room, but as soon as the alterations focused on the old flagstone floor, its atmosphere changed, and one particular flagstone collected a permanent puddle underneath. The source of the water was never traced, and many years later Jean Rowlinson is still convinced that she somehow 'upset' the house with the changes she instigated. The room is now rarely used.

When the Rowlinsons first moved into Bowshaw House, they were told of an old legend concerning the White Lady of Bowshaw, who is said to walk across the lawn and up the portico steps into the entrance hall on certain nights of the year. The identity of the White Lady, in her long flowing dress, has long since been forgotten. Although she has not been seen for many years, it would seem that she walks a very old route, as the entrance into the hallway is an original part of the house dating from the 1730's.

However, hauntings at Bowshaw House and its neighbouring Bowshaw Farm are not limited to the White Lady alone; over the past twenty years, both the Rowlinsons, and their neighbours John and Janice Layton (who lived at Bowshaw Farm until in May 1995), have had a variety of strange experiences. Janice Layton's mother often stayed at the Farm, always in the end bedroom which was only accessible by walking through the other bedrooms, which were interlinked, presumably from the days when this area was reserved for staff. One night she was awoken by a dark female figure who appeared to be standing at the foot of her bed. The following morning, she asked her daughter why she had come into the bedroom on the previous night... to find that nobody had entered the room at all. It was only then that the lady realised that she had not heard any doors open or close.

The Laytons' daughter Joanna returned to the Farm for a short stay over the Christmas of 1994, while she and her husband were waiting for their new house to be completed. The couple were asleep in what had once been Joanna's bedroom, the very end room, when Joanna was woken by the sound of the door handle rattling. She looked towards it and saw that it was turning rapidly, and her first thought was that her sister, who was asleep in the next room, was trying to get in. Joanna climbed out of bed and tried to open the door, which was stuck firm as though somebody were holding it closed from the other side. She briefly let go, and when she took hold of the handle again it opened... to reveal her sister soundly asleep in bed on the other side!

Before the Laytons moved into Bowshaw Farm, they had been told by its former owner, a farm manager, that he had walked into the house one day to see the bathroom door handle rapidly turning itself around, although there was nobody else inside. His wife also felt that a room at the back of the house, which was used as a utility room, had a strange chilling atmosphere... although the Laytons, similar to their neighbours at Bowshaw House, felt that the building was overall a very friendly place, despite their experiences.

The only thing which divides the House from the Farm is a wall which was constructed in the kitchen, at the time of the Hatfield family feud in the 1940's. Half of the kitchen remained on the side of the House, the other is on the side of the Farm. Jean Rowlinson feels that a certain archway in the wall was the most likely route of access between the kitchens, and both she and her son Andrew have experienced a gentle 'brush' of air pass them on many occasions over the years, in the direction of the archway. In the summer of 1995, the Laytons' daughter Joanna was sitting in Jean's kitchen with her back to the Aga stove when she too felt something pass her, brushing her arm gently. Jean has also noted on several occasions that a particularly old wooden cupboard here fills with the smell of methane gas, which disappears quite suddenly. On the other side of the separating wall, the Laytons' dog has often glanced up into one corner of the kitchen as though watching something which the human eyes in the room cannot see. Both families have noted that certain small objects frequently disappear, from bedroom slippers to sets of kitchen knives. Some reappear a while later, others remain lost for good!

Bowshaw House was put up for sale recently, and the Rowlinsons showed round an interested party who paused at the bottom of the stairs and asked whether the house was haunted. When Jean replied that she believed it was, the gentleman replied: 'I know: the ghost just passed me on the stairs!'

Oakwood Hall

Oakwood Hall, in Rotherham, was believed to be one of the grandest houses erected in the city in Victorian times. Businessman James Yates was an iron and steel baron, born in Masborough in 1798. Having owned a number of large Rotherham properties as his business expanded, it was in 1856 that Yates decided to build his own... and purchased the local Lawtons Farm, beginning the construction of Oakwood Hall on the land immediately.

Roche Abbey, scene of many a ghostly encounter.

Before the Hall was finished, a fire broke out and gutted certain rooms of the incomplete building. Yates had to wait longer than he had anticipated to move in, but by 1859 the Hall was repaired and complete. He lived there for just over twenty years before his death. Yates' son had died in tragic barge accident many years earlier, although his daughter Elizabeth was eventually to inherit Oakwood Hall, and resided there with her husband for several years.

Oakwood was sold in the 1890's, and remained a family home until 1916 when work began to convert it into a Rehabilitation Centre for injured ex-servicemen. During this period it was again damaged by a sudden outbreak of fire, and closed soon afterwards... to be converted yet again, this time into a TB sanatorium. Today it is still used by the Health Service, as part of Rotherham District General Hospital.

The history of the building has been so varied that most people are not aware of its many uses throughout this century. In the late 1970's, a local security guard was on his rounds one night when he saw a gentleman making his way towards him along one of the corridors. Concerned that security regulations were being breached, the guard approached the gentleman, and clearly saw his World War I uniform... before he vanished into thin air.

The security guard ran away in terror and never returned to his post. Indeed, until several years after the incident, he had no idea that Oakwood Hall had once been used as a soldiers' Rehabilitation Centre.

Hickleton and The Skulls

Hickleton is a small picturesque village in the Rotherham area, close to Thurnscoe. The east wall of the old hall can be seen from the main street running through the village, which incorporates stone mullioned windows and includes part of the earlier Elizabethan hall. The existing hall is 18th century in origin, and is today a Sue Ryder Home. Whoever haunts the hall remains a mystery, but even the more down-to-earth among the cleaning staff swear that they have felt and heard a presence, and heard the voices of children unknown playing in rooms which, when checked, are empty.

Hickleton Churchyard contains the remains of a medieval cross-base; records survive which show that a church has existed here since at least the early 12th century. The church has its own most unusual feature, in the small stone gateway porch at the front entrance. Three human skulls, believed to be those of highwaymen who were hanged several centuries ago, are on display. Protected by a glass screen, they were set into the brickwork in the 1800's, as a gruesome reminder of their fate.

The Grange, Eckington

A local newspaper report of 1905 noted that Eckington, an ancient Derbyshire parish just beyond Sheffield, was 'until a few years ago a very ancient village. In bygone days it was approached by crossing only wild and rugged moors, cut by ravines, densely wooded on each bank, where wild beasts were yelling, and the timid shrank back afraid.' In later years it became a base for the Sitwell family, who can date their pedigree back to 1301, and are still major landowners in the area. In the summer of 1697 the intrepid traveller Celia Fiennes noted that the Inn she stayed at in Achington was a 'poor, sorry one' and was somewhat put off by the steep Derbyshire hills.

Modern Eckington may be very different in appearance from its sparse and rugged past, but it still displays many fine old buildings, and streets such as Southgate hark back to times when entry to the village would have been guided along slightly different routes than those in use today. Two of the Sitwell sisters owned property, in the last century, on Southgate itself, close to The Grange, now a residential home for the elderly where the following tale is based.

In the late 1980's, Susan Herbert was a regular volunteer at The Grange old people's home on Southgate, and along with a team of other helpers, often supervised jumble-sales and other charity events to raise funds. On one particular occasion, she was lifting boxes of jumble from a downstairs room up a flight of stairs into storage, with the help of a colleague. The two women chatted away as they moved the boxes, with Susan leading the way up the stairs each time. They had done several runs when Susan noticed that her companion had become very quiet, although she could still hear her breathing clearly, and feel her close behind as she made her way up the stairs. When they reached the top, Susan turned around... to find nobody there.

Curious as to why her friend had suddenly doubled back down the stairs without saying a word, she made her way back down, to find that her colleague had not budged from the spot, and Susan had been talking to thin air! Aside from the presence on the stairs, an unexplained smell often appears in various rooms and corridors at Eckington Grange, sometimes in the middle of the night: frying bacon, although nobody can locate the source!

Feoffees

In 1776, the Feoffees of the Common Lands of Rotherham decided to set up a charity school for the less fortunate in the area. As schooling for the young was not enforced until the later Education Acts, Feoffees Charity School provided opportunities for those who would otherwise have remained for the most part uneducated. The school continued as an independent body until its closure in 1892, when the effects of the Education Act came to Rotherham. The old stone-built property passed through several hands over the following century, being used alternately as a dancing school, a vehicle depot and a meeting hall.

When renovations began in the early 1980's, workmen had to break into the cellar from above, as its original entrance had been blocked. Foreman Dave Murphy was the first to be convinced that something lurked in the cellar. He was always the first to arrive and last to leave the site, and had to go into one corner of the building to switch on the lights. He noted at the time: 'The hair on the back of my neck tends to prickle a bit and I get a funny feeling there is something in the air which it not quite answerable to the layman.'

On one occasion, Mr Murphy saw a bright, glowing shape by the top of the cellar stairs, which was about four feet in height. It disappeared on his approach. Thinking that he had possibly seen the headlights of an oncoming vehicle through the window, Mr Murphy checked outside... and realised that the street was one-way and it would not have been feasible. He later noted: 'A sound had attracted my attention, but it wasn't rats because I know there aren't any here. I know whatever it was I saw was about four feet high, because it was slightly taller than the bar we have just put in... I don't believe in these things at all, but I did see something and even talking about it makes my neck prickle.' Rumours of a phantom child, mistreated in the old school, soon began to circulate, although Mr Murphy added of his own sighting: 'I couldn't say it was a child or even a human figure, I don't know what it was.'

Brampton-en-le-Morthen

Brampton was recorded in the time of the Confessor as having three Saxon Lords; Artor, Morcar and Ulchil. When the surveyors came to assess the land of Brampton, they found very little of value and much 'waste' land. Freeholders occupied the area, which was unusual for a period in history when most villagers were the vassals of a local lord. The name of this historic Rotherham village betrays its turbulent past: Morthen means 'killing fields', and during the Civil War, battles were fought in and around the area.

There are three manor houses in the village despite its being considered small in its modern context, and several old stone cottages of 17th and 18th century origin. In one such house, an unwelcome visitor has caused trouble for the Rider family, who have occupied their cottage for around eight years.

Disturbances began with footsteps which walked across the landing as though shod feet were crossing bare wooden floorboards - despite the area over which they 'walked' being carpeted. The Riders' young daughter was only three years old when she began to ask her mother why 'the little old lady' appeared in her bedroom from time to time. Each time their daughter asked this question, the smell of cigarette smoke seemed to emanate from the little girl's bedroom. None of the family smoked, and on one occasion, Corrine Rider was so distressed to smell smoke again that she voiced her complaint out loud. Within a short while, the smell of smoke had been replaced by the scent of an old fashioned rose pot-pourri. The Riders, who are asthmatic, have never used pot-pourri.

Mr Rider remained sceptical about events in the house, and his wife was never frightened, only mystified. In an attempt to look for a possible explanation, she tried to go back into the history of the village, and their house in particular. Sadly, there is very little surviving documentation about Brampton-en-le-Morthen. Although it seemed that the cottage could once have been a farm outbuilding, it is not clear when it was converted into living accomodation. The Riders had themselves undertaken renovation work which altered the position of the kitchen. When phantom smells of cooking lamb (which nobody in the house eats) and baking bread began shortly later, these seemed to emanate from the area of the house which was once the old kitchen.

Lately, however, the disturbances have accelerated somewhat. In 1993, a loud crash in the dining room brought Corrine Rider running to see what had caused the noise. She was amazed to find a heavy wooden sideboard, which has a glass display case filled with Wedgwood china eggs, at the other side of the room turned upside down. Amazingly, none of the eggs inside was broken. Then, in 1994, a beautiful glass candelabra was found smashed on the floor, although moments previously it had been sitting in the centre of the dining table. The atmosphere in the dining room had become unusually cold and unpleasant, and

Corrine Rider remarked that this was the first occasion that the 'presence' had ever damaged anything... and duly warned it that it would 'have to go' if this was ever repeated. Since then, there has been relatively little to report - either the forces responsible have listened to the warning, or they are merely laying low for a while.

St John's Church, Carlton-in-Lindrick

This Anglo-Saxon building, close to the South Yorkshire/North Nottinghamshire border, has several unusual features which make Carlton well worth a visit both for those who believe in legends and those with an interest in early architecture. The tower is Anglo-Saxon, but the belfry was added in the 15th century. Underneath the western belfry window there is an unusual feature of herringbone stonework, where slabs of stone are interwoven in the same style as traditional herringbone fabric.

A 'sun stone' is set above the vestry door in the south aisle, which depicts and sun, moon and stars - slightly pagan in feel for the interior of a church, so it comes as no surprise that a crude cross was cut into it at some point in history.

Carlton hosts its own Devil stone, and it is said that if a visitor runs around it seven times, he or she will either experience good fortune or see the Devil himself. This all depends on which way the stone is circled; clockwise (deosil) will bring good luck, whereas anticlockwise (widdershins) will conjure the Devil. Stones such as this are common throughout England, often featuring in very similar legends. The clockwise versus anticlockwise notion is another common superstition, and recalls old beliefs connected with white and black magic. Local legend also suggests that a white lady haunts the site of the stone, which has been connected with a long-forgotten human sacrifice.

Firbeck Hall

The historic Rotherham village of Firbeck is home to the beautiful Firbeck Hall, once a personal retreat of the old Prince of Wales before his abdication and marriage. Tales of the Green Lady of Firbeck Hall, as featured in *Pit Ghosts, Padfeet and Poltergeists*, are legendary in the area, although her identity remained a mystery to me until local historian Ernest Baker was able provide the following details, which would seem to complete the story:

'During the Civil War, in the middle of the 17th century, the Hall was occupied by a Royalist family called West. One of the daughters was a beautiful girl in her teens. But, to the daughter, politics were much less than love, and she adored a young Roundhead Captain of Cromwell's army, whose name was Galley Knight. Late at night they would meet secretly on the Dark Walk, a path overhung with yew trees to the East of the Hall. Somehow their secret was betrayed, and one night when the young Roundhead arrived at the appointed trysting place he found not his lady-love, but her angry brother, sword in hand.

'When the girl arrived, the body of her lover was lying on the pathway. She was so overcome by grief that she threw herself into the nearby lake. Her body was recovered the next day, mantled in a green shroud of slime and weeds.'

Although the Green Lady is traditionally seen walking from the lake to the shore, Mr Baker also recounted a further story which shows that this was not always the case. This tale dates from the time when Firbeck Hall was opened as a Country Club in the late 1930's. One night after the Club had closed, a young pageboy ran shrieking into the dining room where the staff were having supper. He told of seeing a woman 'dressed in green' coming towards him along an upstairs corridor, who vanished suddenly. A porter reported the same experience two nights later.

Visitor to the Hall Mr O. Hamilton, a London band-leader, was awoken at 2.00 am one morning by a knock on his bedroom door. He opened it to find nobody there, and noted later: 'I closed the door and then I heard the most frightening wailing from the corridor. It was high-pitched and sounded like a woman. I was so scared. The noise was so strange - human, yet not human. I could not move. In the morning I was inclined to laugh it off, until I heard the story of the Green Lady.'

Hauntings at Firbeck Hall have not been restricted to the Green Lady alone; many of the residential staff in the 1930's and '40's were awoken in the middle of the night by the sound of a ghostly tolling bell. Each person who heard it thought that it came from a different direction. The only bells in the building were on the rood of the Hall and on the back wall, although they were so stiff and rusted from disuse that it was felt these could not possibly be the cause. The tolling bell continued to wake sleeping staff between midnight and 2.00 am, usually ringing for a couple of minutes on each occasion. The source of the sounds was never located.

The Tickhill Stage Coach

The historic Doncaster village of Tickhill, resplendent with its own 12th century castle, is reached via equally ancient stretches of road which cut through the fields surrounding it. It is more than likely that some of these roads were once medieval trade routes, which were improved in the last two centuries for regular use by coach and horses. The following story concerns one such road, known as Wong Lane.

On a crystal clear, cold winter evening in the mid-1960's, Trevor Beever was driving along Wong Lane, Tickhill, returning home after playing at a late dance in Doncaster. In the distance he saw, travelling along the railway embankment, what appeared to be the silhouette of an old-fashioned railway carriage with dimly lit windows. Surprised at the antiquity of its shape, and indeed the lack of any engine sound, Mr Beever looked more closely. He was amazed to see the silent vehicle illuminated by the moonlight was not a railway carriage at all, but a stage coach pulled by horses. The coach disappeared from vision behind a large tree... and did not reappear on the other side.

On returning home, Mr Beever told his wife of his strange experience. For almost twenty years, neither of them thought any more about it... until two friends of Mrs Beever told how they too had seen a phantom stage coach travelling along Wong Lane one moonlit night, before it vanished into thin air.

Other Phantom Vehicles

Not simply restricted to ghostly stage coaches, the list of phantom vehicles is endless. Some witnesses have reported buses which vanish in the middle of the road, and lorries and cars which whiz around corners only to disappear from sight and leave no trace as they re-enact fatal accidents on the anniversary of a particularly unpleasant crash. One such sighting occurred in the 1950's in the Brocco Bank area of Sheffield, when two witnesses walking home late at night were horrified to see an obviously out-of-control car veering round a corner past them. A loud crash followed, and the couple ran as fast as they could to the site of the accident to find a hole completely smashed in a stone wall... but no trace of any vehicle. Visibly shaken by the experience, which they reported to local police, they were amazed to find that several other reports of the phantom 'accident' had been given, despite the fact that it had happened

126

two years previously, and the wreckage of the car had long since been removed.

Doncaster woman Mary Banks told how her father had arrived home one night particularly shaken, and recounted an episode which had occurred that evening as he returned from a shooting trip close to where he lived. As the dusk was beginning to fall, her father was travelling along a road between open fields, flanked by hedges. A car without headlights appeared in front of him, crossing the field and passing through two hedges without disturbing them and without making a sound! Mrs Banks pointed out that, some years later, her father was in fact killed by a lorry which hit him on a country road while he was involved in conversation with a farmer. He was returning from a shooting trip at the time.

Perhaps he had had some kind of premonition concerning a strange incident on the road which was an indication of his later death; Mary herself had indeed had a premonitory dream concerning this very incident several weeks before her father's death.

Whiston Church

Whiston was once a busy village on part of a major road which spanned the North of England. The historian Joseph Hunter noted: 'The roads from Sheffield to Tickhill and from Rotherham to Mansfield, which was formerly one of the greatest highways to the North of England, intersect each other near the village of Whiston.' In the mid-1800's a fine hoard of Roman coins was found here, indicating that the area had been settled for several centuries. Today, Whiston is a quiet Rotherham village which is considered rather more off the beaten track than would once have been so.

In 1947, a young Rotherham musician named Trevor Beever was a regular visitor to the old Church at Whiston, whose pipe organ he used on a regular basis. Mr Beever had been given a key to the building so that he could enter and leave at will, enabling him to practice during the evening when services were not in progress. One such winter evening, Mr Beever unlocked the church as normal and began to practise alone. Most of the church was in darkness, as he was in the habit of only using necessary lighting over the organ itself.

When he heard the sound of footsteps moving along the centre of the church on the stone floor, Mr Beever turned to see who had entered the

WORTLEY HALL.

building... and saw no one. Puzzled, he left his seat and walked towards the small room which was at this time used to house the choristers' garments and other materials. He heard the door click as it opened and closed, although he could still see nobody. Warily, Mr Beever followed the mysterious footsteps into the small room, which was in darkness. He called out, but received no reply, and suddenly became aware of a strange chill enveloping him. Despite admitting to being slightly sceptical in nature, he left the church as quickly as he could and swore never to practice there again alone on dark winter evenings!

On telling his story, other frequenters of Whiston Church offered 'rational' explanations in the form of creaking pews and old heating pipes. And yet, others came forward who had still experienced the same inexplicable footsteps and chilled atmosphere for themselves.

Catling-Hall

The Peak town of Penistone on the South Yorkshire/Derbyshire border took its name from 'the ton on the pen', meaning 'town on the hilltop'. Held by the Saxon Ailric both before and after the Conquest, Penistone passed into the hands of his son on his death. Catling-Hall was built in the 16th century, taking its name from the family who resided there.

Although little is known of them, their name can be seen on early charters from the Penistone area. Catling-Hall later became a home for the Sotwells, who at one time included the Vicar of Penistone among their number. At some point in the last hundred years, its name altered to Cathill Hall.

Frank Henry Gaunt was once a familiar figure outside Cathill Hall. He would lay food down to encourage the foxes, so that the local hunt had an abundance of quarry on its seasonal outings. Donald Nutbrown was a small boy at the time, and would often help Mr Gaunt in his work. They were outside the Hall one afternoon, when a gentleman in Edwardian dress appeared from the direction of Gunthwaite Hall and walked past them both in the direction of Penistone. He offered no greeting and appeared not to have noticed either of them, although Donald was curious as to his clothing and asked Mr Gaunt who the gentleman was. Mr Gaunt replied that the figure appeared only at certain times each year and walked the same route - he was not a living person, but a ghost! His identity had been lost with the passage of time, but Mr Gaunt was used to his appearances and felt no fear.

At one time, the old public footpath which ran past Cathill Hall was used in the transportation of prisoners going from the feared Halifax Gaol to the Gaol at Sheffield. Cathill Hall itself was a stop-off point, and was equipped with secure holding places for the criminals while their guards rested inside. Conditions for transporting prisoners were notoriously bad in the last century, and it is likely that many died on the trail as they made the long and treacherous journey in all weather conditions. Frank Henry Gaunt told Donald Nutbrown that at certain times, he had heard the sounds of ghostly rattling chains carried on the wind over the moors.

Beauchief Abbey

Beauchief Abbey was founded by Robert Fitz Ranulf de Alfreton, the lord of Norton and various manors in Derbyshire. He oversaw its foundations being laid in the early 1200's, and legend has it that his eagerness to build such a wonderful house of God stems from his part in the murder of Thomas à Becket earlier on in that decade: building the Abbey was part of his penance.

Along with the generosity of other local lords, who gave cattle fields and cornmills and other offerings, the White Canons who entered the

Beauchief Abbey

order appear to have been very well looked after. The site of their ancient corn mill in Sheffield is today remembered as Millhouses.

Only the 12th century west tower of Beauchief Abbey remains standing today. There are rumours that underground passages riddle the local terrain, and some researchers into the paranormal have suggested that the Abbey is built along ancient lines of earth power known as ley lines. This may not be such an unusual idea, since many of the older churches and abbeys all over the country are felt to have been built on over sites of natural power, once used by practitioners of the old religion.

A mysterious White Lady has been seen flitting in and out of the ruins of Beauchief Abbey, along with a hooded monk whom some say has a skeleton for a face. The legend of the underground tunnels was noted by Addy in his collection of local folklore tales. In such a tunnel between the Abbey and Norton Church, it is said that a metal box exists containing great treasure, which must be approached by riding a backward-shod white horse into the passageway. From hereon, the adventurer may open the box, which will reveal untold-of delights!

The Thorpe Hesley Boggard

'Boggard' is a regional term used frequently earlier in the century to describe an apparition which appears from time to time at a certain location. In the case of the Thorpe Hesley Boggard, it also coined its own regional saying: 'Tha comes and goes like the Thorpe Hesley Boggard!' The story behind this apparition is difficult to trace, having somewhat died out this century, but could have something to do with the tale of the death of the local Earl of Strafford, who was beheaded on Tower Hill in 1641.

In a Christmas Eve edition of the *Rotherham Advertiser*, dated 1942, local historian Dr Gilbert Mould recounted: 'During the forty-three years I have lived at the Grange [Kimberworth] I have been familiar with the legend that the Earl of Strafford at certain times walked down Haigh Lane from Wentworth Woodhouse carrying his head under his arm. At these times they used to say that the children would not go to school.'

The last recorded sighting of the Earl with his head under his arm was at the turn of the century. An ancient oak tree, which marked the spot from where the Earl was taken for execution on that fateful day in 1641, until comparatively recently stood in Tankersley Park, and was known as 'Earl Strafford's Oak'. It is said that after his execution on May 12, at which a crowd of many thousands of people gathered, the Earl was interred at an unmarked grave in Hooton Roberts. His widow retreated to a house in this village, and requested that she too be buried without a headstone. Whatever the truth of this tale, no recent sightings of the Thorpe Hesley Boggard have been reported, as he carries his head under his arm while retracing his last steps.

Final Words

Many think of South Yorkshire as an industrial county, peopled by down-to-earth Northern folk who have no time for superstition and legend. Far from being the case, the county possesses many pubs, collieries, shops, churches and even council houses which are reputedly haunted... and as for tales of fairies, witches and UFO's, there are obviously more around who believe in these things than would at first admit! Despite its industrial image, South Yorkshire is rich with historic buildings whose corridors still echo with romantic tales of tragic deaths, and the sound of ghostly footsteps...

A fearful apparition!

Publisher's Postscript:

I have never, to the best of my knowledge, seen or encountered a ghost. I may have felt one or two. Being a child of a seventh child (though not quite the seventh son of a seventh son) I should perhaps be more susceptible to these things, but my psychic feelings have been mainly confined to the odd occasion when I knew what was going to happen next. Unfortunately, so far in my life, this has never happened at a racetrack. However, a couple of odd things happened while I was editing this book that left me at least stirred, if not shaken, and I thought I would share them with the reading public to show that — however much we think we've gotten it all buttoned up and accounted for — sometimes the universe contains an odd grain of the unexpected ...

While editing this book I have occasionally worked late, through the night. This does not bother me unduly. I stick the radio on, open a bottle of wine, and can quite happily edit until two or three in the morning until natural tiredness overtakes me. This particular night in question I had been editing the poltergeist parts of the book, to do with the light bulbs blowing. I finished my stint, sent it to the printer, and turned in for the night. I work from home, so it was only a matter of going next door. After the usual ablutions, I settled down in bed. I must have nodded off with the light on. Like most people of the "hippy" generation, I tend to favour those large white circular paper globe type lampshades - I'm sure you know the sort.

When I awoke next morning, the light was out, but the switch on the wall was still pressed "on". The light bulb had been *unscrewed* from its socket and was wedged in the wire at the bottom of the lightshade, hanging downwards towards the floor!

A few days after this I had just about got my head round the fact that perhaps the light bulb hadn't been very securely fitted in the first place and had somehow managed to work loose and fall in such a way that it wedged itself in the wire at the bottom of the lightshade, and it was all, thus, suddenly explicable, when the following happened.

I was leaving an industrial estate in South Yorkshire - which will be nameless, though it does in fact have its own tradition of being haunted by a headless monk - and it was early evening. Dark, autumn definitely here, whatever the forecasters said. As I drove down the long, straight empty road that connected this area with the rest of civilisation, a black shape, darker than its surroundings, detached itself from the rest of the vestigial gloom and "coalesced" in my headlights. That is the only word I can use to describe the eerie way it became solid even as my eyes perceived it. It was a huge (capital H) black dog. It took no notice whatsoever of my presence driving towards it, but casually loped over the road out of my headlights and onto a path at the right hand edge of the estate entrance.

I thought, laughingly, to myself, "at last, a real live Padfoot". Then the idea occurred to me that it might be someone's pet, lost, so I stopped my van, got out, and took a few hesitant steps towards the path. It was less than 30 seconds since I had seen it, there was nowhere for it to go: I started up the path, hoping to entice whatever it was to come back. Needless to say, it had vanished ...

STEVE RUDD

Bibliography

The following books provided historical background for several of the stories included in *More Pitghosts, Padfeet And Poltergeists:*

Kerr, N & M.A *Guide to Anglo-Saxon Sites*, Paladin
Johnson *Folk Memory*, Oxford (Clarendon Press)
Addy, S. O. *Folk Tales & Superstitions*
Marsden, B. *The Early Barrow Diggers*, Shire Publications Ltd
Hunter, J. *South Yorkshire* Vols. I & II, JB Nicholls & Son
Turner & Sass *The Eckington Files*, Chesterfield Arts Centre
Tilley *Old Halls, Manors & Families of Derbyshire*
Potter-Briscoe, J. *Notts & Derbys at Opening of XX Century*, Pike
Shaw, G.A *Brief History of Eckington*, Eckington & District Preservation Society
Kemp, A. *Witchcraft & Paganism Today*, Michael O'Mara
Clarke, D. *Ghosts and Legends of the Peak District* Jarrold

Also used were past editions of *The Barnsley Chronicle, The Rotherham Advertiser, The Sheffield Telegraph, The Sun, Derbyshire Now* Magazine, and *The Sheffield Star*.

Acknowledgements

I would like to thank the following people for their help:

David Clarke, for kindly contributing a foreword, Morgaine Bailey, Ed Law, Ernest Baker, Dinnington Local History Library, Maisie Robson, Julie Thompson for the Padfoot drawing, John Brailsford, Ian Worthington and in addition all the contributors, too numerous to mention individually, who were willing to tell me their stories.